PENGUIN HANDBOOKS

The Walker's Handbook

Hugh Westacott was born in London in 1932 and moved to Epsom, Surrey, on the outbreak of the war. He was educated at Tiffin Boys' School, Kingston-upon-Thames, and the Northwestern Polytechnic. He is at present the Deputy County Librarian of Buckinghamshire and has also worked as a librarian in Sutton, Croydon, Sheffield, Bradford and Brookline, Massachusetts. During the war, he spent his holidays with his family in Colyton, East Devon, walking five miles to the sea and back again each day, and his love of walking stems from these experiences.

Among his other publications are *A Practical Guide to Walking the Ridgeway Path*, *A Practical Guide to Walking the Devon South Coast Path* and *A Practical Guide to Walking the Dorset Coast Path*. His other interests are writing footpath guides, the history of the Royal Navy in the eighteenth century and the novels of Evelyn Waugh. Hugh Westacott is married and has two daughters.

D0774297

H. D. WESTACOTT

The Walker's Handbook

PENGUIN BOOKS

Penguin Books Ltd, Harmondsworth,
Middlesex, England
Penguin Books, 625 Madison Avenue,
New York, New York 10022, U.S.A.
Penguin Books Australia Ltd, Ringwood,
Victoria, Australia
Penguin Books Canada Ltd, 2801 John Street,
Markham, Ontario, Canada L3R 1B4
Penguin Books (N.Z.) Ltd, 182–190 Wairau Road,
Auckland 10, New Zealand

First published 1978
Reprinted 1979
Copyright © Hugh Douglas Westacott, 1978
All rights reserved

Made and printed in Great Britain by
Hazell Watson & Viney Ltd, Aylesbury, Bucks
Set in Monotype Baskerville

For the best of companions

CONTENTS

LIST OF FIGURES

ACKNOWLEDGEMENTS

An author who brings together in one book information which is widely scattered and not readily available must rely heavily on the goodwill of many people to make his task easier. I could not have wished for more helpful informants. So many people have helped me that it is not possible to acknowledge all my sources but particular thanks are due to the following: to Miss Teresa Way, who has typed the manuscript twice and coped admirably with my eccentric handwriting; to my friends Joe Lowrey and Miss Doris Bonwitt, who read the original manuscript and made many constructive criticisms; to the Countryside Commission, especially the Senior Cartographer, Mr J. Crawforth, for supplying among other things a great deal of information about map numbers and for permitting the reproduction of maps of long-distance footpaths, National Parks and Areas of Outstanding Natural Beauty; to Mr D. H. McPherson, Honorary Secretary of the Scottish Rights of Way Society Ltd, for helpful comments on the chapter dealing with the law relating to rights of way in Scotland; to the Countryside Commission for Scotland for providing information; to Silva Compass (London) Ltd, for permission to reproduce an illustration of a Silva compass; to the County Planning Officers of Avon, Bedfordshire, Berkshire, Buckinghamshire, Cornwall, Cumbria, Devon, Dorset, East Sussex, Essex, Gloucestershire, Gwent, Gwynedd, Hampshire, Hereford and Worcester, Hertfordshire, Humberside, Isle of Wight, Kent, Lancashire, Lincolnshire, Norfolk, North Yorkshire, Northumberland, Oxfordshire, Salop, Somerset, Staffordshire, Suffolk, Surrey, West Glamorgan, West Sussex and Wiltshire for supplying information about Areas of Outstanding Natural Beauty; to my friends and colleagues the County Librarians of Avon, Berkshire, Cornwall, Cumbria, Devon, Dorset, Dyfed, East Sussex, Essex, Gloucestershire, Gwent, Gwynedd, Hampshire, Hereford and Worcester, Humberside, Isle of Wight, Lancashire, Lincolnshire, Norfolk, Northumberland, Oxfordshire, Salop, Staffordshire, Suffolk, Surrey, West Glamorgan, West Sussex and Wiltshire for tracing and producing bibliographical information about footpath guides in National Parks and Areas of Outstanding Natural Beauty.

And finally, my special thanks to my wife and daughters for their tolerance and forbearance during the gestation period of this book.

INTRODUCTION

The last few years have seen a great revival of interest in walking for recreation, encouraged in part by the energy crisis and the growing concern with the quality of the environment. It is a curious fact that although there are a number of excellent books written about walking there is not one moderately priced book which treats the subject comprehensively. This is an attempt to fill that gap. It is about all kinds of walking, from ambling through lowland pastures to tramping the tops of the Lake District. It is about walking only; it does not cover any aspect of climbing. Those who want to know about anything that involves ropes, karabiners or pitons must look elsewhere. Whenever the word 'climbing' is used in this book it must be understood to mean 'ascending'.

Although written particularly with the novice walker in mind, this should prove a useful book of reference for the more experienced, as it contains a great deal of information not readily available elsewhere. In particular, the extensive bibliography and the information given about Ordnance Survey sheet numbers and footpath guides for the long-distance paths, National Parks and Areas of Outstanding Natural Beauty should prove helpful. I hope, too, that visitors from overseas will find it useful and they should be able to find within its covers most of the essential information they require.

Walkers tend to be individualists and we all have our fads, fancies, prejudices, likes and dislikes, so let me declare mine now, so that those who read on may make allowances for them. My particular love is for the mountains and fells of the Lake District and the Pennines. At present, I am exiled to Buckinghamshire and am forced, therefore, to walk in the lowlands, which nevertheless I enjoy a great deal.

While I am delighted that many people are discovering the gentle pleasures of walking, I am uneasy about some of the activities of the Countryside Commission, National Park Boards and other official bodies. Waymarking, wardens, nature trails, picnic sites and toilets may seem perfectly reasonable in themselves but they do smack of regimentation.

There will always be the people who want to follow their own paths and this book is written for them. Much of it contains guidance and suggestions only, based on the experience of many walkers. In the course of time, the reader may wish to follow his own inclinations and walk in the manner that suits him. That is all to the good, for there are only three rules from which the walker must never depart:

(1) Follow the Country Code
(2) Always obey the law
(3) Be properly equipped for the mountains and fells

At the end of each chapter will be found suggestions for further reading. Most of these books may be obtained from the public library and, if your particular interest is not included, your public librarian will be able to recommend and obtain suitable titles for you.

I have tried to ensure that all the information contained in this book was correct on 28 February 1977.

THE PLEASURES OF
WALKING

After breathing, walking is probably the most basic human activity, and a person who, for whatever reason, is unable to walk is regarded as severely handicapped. Almost everybody *can* walk, but the way in which each person walks varies enormously. There is all the difference in the world between the businessman hurrying tensely and purposefully to the station fearing that his train might have left and the walker slowly ascending a mountain path filling his lungs with unpolluted air and revelling in the magnificent scenery around him. Yet both are putting one foot in front of the other.

Already we have hit on one of the clues to walking for pleasure. Many people delight in beautiful scenery and there is no doubt that the best way to enjoy and experience the countryside is to walk in it. Those who see the countryside from the inside of a car miss so much. Roads rarely follow the most scenic routes, but footpaths nearly always do. Roadside verges always stink of petrol fumes, whereas two hundred yards away over the stile it is possible to smell the wild fragrance of the countryside.

Walking combines well with other interests. The naturalist has to walk quietly through the landscape to avoid disturbing wildlife and even the casual walker is likely to see things he will remember for a long time. Some of my special memories are of watching buzzards soaring effortlessly from the Cheviots, seeing a vixen carrying a rabbit back to her cubs, almost stepping on a fox in a ditch very early in the morning, and watching three young weasels playing tag around an oak tree. One walk near Malham in Yorkshire was made memorable by a botanist friend showing me tiny alpine flowers growing in the clefts of the limestone.

The landscape itself is a fascinating study. Although the shape of the mountains, hills, streams and valleys pre-dates man, yet man has largely created the British landscape. He has cut down the primeval forest, drained the land and enclosed the fields with a complicated pattern of hedges, walls and ditches. The animals that he has grazed, the crops he has sown, the trees he has felled, the valleys he has drained or flooded for reservoirs – all have an effect on the ecology of the landscape.

In the course of moulding the landscape, man built towns and villages. Discovering the reasons for siting settlements in particular places makes an interesting detective puzzle for the curious to unravel. The walker has time to admire the natural taste and eye for beauty shown by our ancestors in building even the humblest dwellings. It is hard to pass by Thwaite in Swaledale, for instance, and not remark on the number of exceptionally elegant stone barns with dovecots to be seen in the fields. Evidence of change, decay and renewal are there for the inquiring walker to discover and interpret. A few miles from my home is a pleasant village that I have driven through many times, but it was not until I walked through it and in the surrounding fields that I noticed that the church stood in an isolated position outside the village. This so intrigued me that I went over to investigate. In the fields around the church were numerous shallow depressions where once houses had stood. I discovered from a visit to the local history library that much of the village had been moved a few hundred yards to a new site and only the church had been left untouched.

It is exciting to discover for oneself traces of the past. A piece of rough land fenced off from an otherwise fertile pasture turns out to be the remains of a motte and bailey castle built by the Normans; a circular barn on a slight bluff is all that is left of an old windmill; that remarkably broad path with a pronounced crown and evidence of ditches on both sides is obviously an old road which may turn out to be prehistoric or Roman, or a forgotten drove road. It is fun, too, to follow old Roman roads from Ordnance Survey maps and it is surprising how many there are for the diligent searcher to find. Those interested in antiquities marked on the Ordnance Survey maps will find that accurate use of the compass is invaluable in pin-pointing the exact location of sites.

There is now a great deal of interest in industrial archaeology and the walker will often observe traces of past industry. The Pennines are particularly rich in old mine workings where lead, iron, silver and other metals and minerals were extracted. Because the workings are often some distance from the nearest settlement, they have frequently remained remarkably intact and it is possible to come across not only mine shafts and levels, but also engine sheds and bits of rusting machinery. The industrial revolution started in the valleys of northern England, where there was abundant water both for power and for cleaning, and some of these early factories still exist as fine buildings in lovely settings. Disused canals, railways and tramways can be found all over the country and are well worth exploring.

Exploring places connected with writers and their work can add an extra dimension to walking. One thinks of the Hardy country in Dorset or, as he called it, Wessex; the Brontë country is near Keighley in West Yorkshire, and the Shakespeare country is Warwickshire. Top Withens, the ruined house generally believed to be the inspiration of *Wuthering Heights* in Emily Brontë's novel, actually lies on the Pennine Way. Arthur Ransome set his books in the Lake District and at Beatrix Potter's home at Far Sawrey near Lake Windermere it is possible to see the vegetable garden where Mr McGregor chased Peter Rabbit and the chimney that Tom Kitten explored. One can have a good long walk over the Berkshire Downs following the journey of the rabbits in Richard Adams' novel, *Watership Down*.

Walking as described in this book is not a competitive sport and is done purely for pleasure. It is an excellent way of keeping fit and can be continued until late into life. There

are many sixty-year-olds and seventy-year-olds who regularly go into the mountains and who can surprise younger,
less-experienced walkers with their strength and stamina.

The novice walker should proceed with some caution,
especially if he has a sedentary job and is unused to exercise.
Make a start by toning up the muscles of the legs and feet by
going barefoot about the house and garden. Take purposeful
strolls along quiet roads, parks and canal paths, covering a
specific distance – say two or three miles at first, working up
to five or six. Once you are able to cover six miles or so without discomfort, you are ready for some real walking and can
plan some circuits on local footpaths. No special clothes or
equipment are necessary for walking in lowland areas,
though most people will find comfortable stout shoes a help,
together with a small rucksack, duffle bag or haversack to
carry sandwiches, a drink and a plastic raincoat. Before trying more ambitious walks on moor and mountain it is essential to have the proper equipment described in Chapter 2.

The walker who has gained some experience and pleasure
from exploring local paths and has become proficient in
map-reading and use of the compass may wish to venture on
a walking holiday. There are many ways of planning walking holidays, some of them suitable for families. Children
are very tough little creatures and providing they have been
properly introduced to walking and enjoy it they should get
a great deal from a walking holiday.

For the beginner, planning such a holiday, it is probably
best to find a suitable centre, stay there for the duration of
the holiday and walk each day. The walks do not necessarily
have to be circular, for, with careful planning, public transport can be used for the journey in one direction. It is usually
more satisfactory and reliable to catch a bus to the starting
point and then walk home, as there is then no danger of
weary members of the party missing the bus or finding it full.
Another advantage of walking from a centre is that trips to
cathedrals, castles, stately homes and other places of interest
can be made on days when the weather is unsuitable for

walking. This type of holiday is particularly good for families with children.

There are many types of accommodation for one-centre walking holidays, ranging from camp sites to five-star hotels. The public library is a mine of information about holidays and accommodation. There are numerous directories of hotels and boarding houses, camp/caravan sites, self-catering holidays and farmhouse accommodation. The better directories give very detailed information about the facilities offered, such as whether pets and children are welcomed.

The public library will also have tourist guides to the area being visited. Among the best if also the most prosaic are the Ward Lock Guides, which often give details of local walks, although they do not pretend to be exhaustive.

There are some organizations, notably the CHA and the Holiday Fellowship as well as some Christian groups, which organize holidays which contain a large amount of walking. Frequently walks are graded for beginners, the more experienced and expert and are led by highly experienced leaders who know the area well. The Youth Hostels Association has a few hostels with family units attached where families can stay for two weeks or so instead of the normal maximum three nights. Many of these organizations are 'dry' and alcoholic drinks are usually forbidden on their premises, so those who want a convivial drink have to go out to the local pub and make the excuse that they are going to watch the sunset!

Some walkers prefer not to stay at one centre but to undertake a walking tour and sleep in a different place every night. This can be very enjoyable but entails some careful planning, especially if there are several in the group. In the wilder parts of the country, where accommodation is sparse, it is advisable to book in advance, especially in the peak season. The question of accommodation can be quite critical and must be investigated properly beforehand, otherwise the walker may find himself in difficulties. For example, the last stage of the Pennine Way is a gruelling twenty-seven miles from Byrness to Kirk Yetholm across the Cheviots, rising to some 2,500 ft. Only the strongest walkers can hope to complete it in one day and then only by starting very early in the morning, so there is very little leeway if the walk is to be finished in daylight hours. The only chance of accommodation is three miles off the route at a shepherd's croft and there is a mountain hut (an old railway truck) some seven miles from Kirk Yetholm. There is no other shelter of any kind.

Bed and breakfast accommodation can be found in most towns and villages at pubs, guest houses and private houses. Not all such places advertise. There seems to be some sort of freemasonry among bed and breakfast establishments whereby if the first is full you are sent on to the next until someone somewhere can put you up. There are several guides to bed and breakfast accommodation which can usually be seen at public libraries. One of the best is the *Bed and Breakfast Guide* published annually by the Ramblers' Association (free to members). The walker can be assured that his special needs will be catered for at the addresses listed in this guide as nobody will mind his muddy attire and there will be facilities for drying sodden clothing. I well remember walking to Greenhead on the Pennine Way. It had poured with rain all day and the last three hours of the downpour had been torrential. It was too wet to camp and so I telephoned someone listed in the *Bed and Breakfast Guide*. When I arrived at the house, my offer to take off my wet clothing outside was indignantly refused and an old piece of carpet obviously kept specially for the purpose was unrolled in the kitchen for me to stand on. My wet clothing was hung up to dry; a bath was drawn for me and in no time at all I was sitting in dry clothes in front of a blazing fire eating a huge supper. My host had been a miner and quarryman for most of his life and I spent a most entertaining evening listening about mining in the Pennines and the miner's life forty years ago.

The Youth Hostels Association, which, despite its name, caters for outdoor people of any age, have hostels offering simple accommodation all over the country. Many of them, especially in the more popular areas, are within walking distance of each other and offer a splendid opportunity for a really inexpensive but not too spartan walking holiday. Membership is £2·00 for adults, with reduced fees for juniors and children. Overnight charges range from 70p to £1·40 for seniors and meals cost 74p for supper and 60p for breakfast. It is also possible to prepare your own meals in the kitchen. Prices are kept low because hostel visitors do a lot of chores such as washing up, preparing vegetables, cleaning etc. The hostels themselves range from the really primitive, like Black Sail, a shepherd's croft in the Lake District, to the almost luxurious. The main disadvantage of youth hostels, especially to the more fastidious, is the communal life. However, many people seem to enjoy them and like sharing their experiences with others.

The type of holiday which offers the walker the greatest flexibility but is also the most arduous is a camping holiday on which he carries his own tent. As whole books have been written about backpacking, here it deserves at least a chapter to itself.

Where to go? One of the United Kingdom's greatest glories is its amazing variety of scenery packed into such a small area. It is possible to go to any rural area and have a splendid holiday exploring the local footpath and bridleway network. As we have seen, walking combines very well with other interests and walkers will have the venue of their holiday dictated by the location of their interest. Chapters 10 and 11 describe all the National Parks and Areas of Outstanding Natural Beauty for those interested primarily in walking in beautiful scenery. In Chapter 12 are described all the long-distance paths created by the Countryside Commission, all of which are suitable for walking holidays, and one can stay at different places every night. But some of them – especially the Pennine Way – are very arduous and suitable only for the experienced fell-walker.

On winter evenings it is fun to examine Ordnance Survey maps to plan new walks and to remember old ones. The place names of Britain are so musical and exciting that they positively invite investigation – Rough Tor, Brown Willy, Sutton Thorn, Downhayne Brake, High Cup Nick, Dolly-waggon Pike, Glaramara, Pike o' Stickle, Ringing Roger, Thunacar Knott, Chanctonbury Ring, Ivinghoe Beacon, Black Sail Pass, Wildboar Clough, Cader Idris, Pen-y-Ghent, Great Whernside, Langstrothdale . . .

Bibliography

AUTOMOBILE ASSOCIATION, *Guide to Guesthouses, Farmhouses and Inns*, published annually by the Automobile Association.

Children Welcome! published annually by Herald Advisory Services.

ENGLISH TOURIST BOARD, *Activity Holidays in England*, Vol. 2, published annually by the English Tourist Board.

Farm Holiday Guide, published annually by Farm Holiday Guides Ltd. (Editions for England, Wales and Scotland)

HILLABY, JOHN, *Journey through Britain*, Constable, 1968.

HOSKINS, W. G., *English Landscapes*, BBC, 1973.

HOSKINS, W. G., *The Making of the English Landscape*, Penguin Books, 1970.

MUNRO, SIR HUGH, *Munro's Tables of the 3,000 Feet Mountains of Scotland, and Other Tables of Lesser Heights*, Scottish Mountaineering Trust, 1974.

RAMBLERS' ASSOCIATION, *Bed and Breakfast Guide*, published annually by the Ramblers' Association.

RAMBLERS' ASSOCIATION and YOUTH HOSTELS ASSOCIATION, *Rambling and Youth Hostelling*, Educational Products, 1967.

SCOTTISH TOURIST BOARD, *Where to Stay in Scotland*, published by the Scottish Tourist Board.

WATKINS, ALFRED, *The Old Straight Track*, 2nd edn, Garnstone Press, 1970.

WRIGHT, NICK, *English Mountain Summits*, Hale, 1974.

2   CLOTHES AND EQUIPMENT

Before choosing clothes and equipment for walking it is as well to have a clear idea of the sort of terrain you are likely to explore. Unless the conditions were to be exceptionally severe, it is unlikely that anyone would ever be in any danger in any lowland part of the southern counties or far from a place from which help could readily be obtained. It is quite different in the mountains and on the moors. Even in the summer months, conditions above 2,000 ft can be appalling and help unobtainable. The novice, sitting in a café in the valley watching the rain gusting in, cannot imagine what it is like on top of the fells. Once, early in September, I was walking the Pennine Way and left Dufton to walk the twenty or so miles to Alston. It was raining gently and there was a strong breeze in the valley, but the higher I climbed the more the wind blew and visibility became poorer. At the top of Great Dun Fell (2,780 ft) is a radar station with several huge masts, but so bad were the conditions that I could see the masts only when I was within twenty yards of them. I had to walk the six miles from Knock Hush to Cross Fell navigating entirely by compass. The wind was so strong that at times I had to bend almost double to force my way along. The local Helm wind was blowing and it would have been wiser to retreat, but there was plenty of shelter along the way and I had a tent, sleeping bag, survival bag and three days' supply of food, so I decided to continue.

Cairns mark the path, but in the thick mist it was impossible to see from one to the next and the rain was drum-

ming on my fell-jacket like hail stones. At the top of Cross
Fell, which is almost 3,000 ft high, the path makes a 90° turn
to meet the old corpse road to Garrigill. There is a trig point
on the top of Cross Fell and I hoped to find it so that I could
use it to take a bearing. Although I knew I was on the summit of Cross Fell because I had passed through the girdle of
rocks which form its outer edge, I was unable to locate the
trig point even though I quartered the summit in a grid
pattern counting my steps so as not to get lost. In the end, I
had to take my compass bearing and walk down the fellside
until I picked up the path. When walking in such conditions
one loses all sense of direction and it is essential to rely on
the compass even though one's instincts may tell one that
the compass points in the wrong direction. If these were the
conditions in early September, imagine what they are like in
the depths of winter!

I have described this walk as it illustrates very clearly the
weather any walker is likely to meet sooner or later on mountains or moorland. Unless properly clad and equipped, the
walker will be in serious danger of dying of exposure. From
time to time, tragic incidents are reported of walkers and
climbers who have succumbed to the rigours of the weather.
Practically all these incidents would not have happened if
those involved had been properly equipped. Less than a
week after walking over Cross Fell I was in Borrowdale in
the Lake District near Sprinkling Tarn, some 2,000 ft up,
when I came across the body of a camper dead beside his
collapsed tent. The police were able to reconstruct the sad
story. He had left Seathwaite on a Saturday afternoon in
early September in driving rain and a howling gale. A
shepherd had stopped him and warned him that he should
not go onto the fells in such conditions. Nevertheless, he
carried on and by the time night fell he was soaked to the
skin. He pitched his tent in the most sheltered spot he could
find, took off all his wet clothes and got into his sleeping bag.
During the night the wind rose to tremendous force (one
shepherd said they were the worst autumn gales he could

remember) and his tent blew down. He was now without any protection except for a heap of stones behind which he tried to shelter. It was too late; although the weather was not cold, the wind and the rain soon sapped his strength and he died of exposure. Had he had with him a survival bag, which is merely a plastic bag large enough to get inside, he would almost certainly have lived to tell the tale.

Exposure occurs when the body temperature cools down to a point where it can no longer support life. It is obvious that this will happen if the body is not protected against extremely low temperature, but it is often not appreciated that exposure can occur in comparatively mild temperatures if the body is not adequately protected against wind and rain. The temperature of the body is controlled by the pores of the skin. Under normal conditions the pores excrete water vapour. When the body is cold, the pores close, and in an attempt to increase warmth by stimulation the body will start to shiver; when too hot, the skin will be flooded by moisture which cools the body by evaporation. Both sweating and shivering are to be avoided whenever possible because in these conditions the body is not at its most efficient and valuable energy is being wasted in an attempt to regulate the temperature.

The properly clad walker, therefore, must wear clothes which will protect him from the elements and at the same time keep his body at an efficient temperature. There are fashions and fads in walking as there are in all sports, and personal preferences play a part, too. I do not like anoraks because I think they are too short in the body and ventilation cannot be controlled adequately. Nevertheless, a good anorak will have all the weatherproof qualities which makes it a suitable garment for walking on the fells. Providing that clothing is chosen on the correct principles, you will still have a choice of gear to suit your own needs. Warmth is induced by trapping layers of air all round the body. Still air is an excellent insulator and it is essential to wear clothes that will trap the air and hold it in place. At the same time it is important that the water vapour given off by the body can escape easily and that it is possible to provide sufficient ventilation to prevent sweating.

These conditions can be met in the following ways. Firstly, put on a string T-shirt, obtainable from specialist sports shops. Next, a lambswool sweater followed by a woollen jacket-length shirt. The nether parts should be clothed in cotton underwear and worsted breeches. It is important that all the above garments except underwear should be of wool because it is both light and warm. Wool will allow water vapour from the body to pass through, it can absorb nearly three times its own weight of water and it will remain warm to the touch even when soaking wet. No synthetic material has these qualities.

In foul weather, rainproof outer garments are required. These may be an anorak, a cagoule (which is really a knee-length anorak), or jacket. I favour the knee-length jacket as it gives the best control over ventilation and can be undone and worn open in between showers. Whatever style is chosen, it should be of the best quality, with all zips and fastenings covered with storm-proof flaps, and have a hood. The most widely used material is polyurethane-covered nylon, which is totally impervious to water when new but will chafe as it ages and become ineffective. Unfortunately, it is not possible to re-proof with polyurethane, although leaking seams can be sealed with clear Bostik. There are various weights of nylon and you should always buy the heaviest available, as lightweight weatherproofs soon lose their resistance to rain and are more likely to tear. A good-quality walking jacket will cost £15 or more. Anoraks and cagoules are a little less expensive. Choose a brightly coloured garment as this will not only be more cheerful to wear in the rain but will enable you to be seen more easily in the event of an accident. When buying equipment always go to a specialist walkers' and climbers' shop – advice will be obtainable from the staff, who are likely to be enthusiasts themselves and have a great deal of practical experience. Avoid chain and army surplus stores.

Canvas or nylon gaiters are at present very fashionable. These attach to the boots and extend to just above the knee. They are extremely useful in showery weather, especially when worn with knee-length jackets or cagoules, and also give good protection against wet vegetation. Some walkers always wear them whatever the weather conditions. In bad weather some form of overtrouser is always necessary. Leggings are better as they allow the crotch to breathe but they are difficult to obtain, so some walkers convert overtrousers. Leggings cannot be worn with anoraks because they do not cover the crotch. Whatever is selected, it should be of polyurethane-coated nylon or neoprene.

Totally impermeable outer clothes will inevitably induce condensation on the inside. Careful design will give as much ventilation as possible, but if you walk all day in pouring rain you will end up damp from condensation. This is a fact of life until technology gives us the ideal material which breathes and yet is totally weatherproof. Nevertheless, it is better to end up warm and damp from condensation (warm wet) than cold and damp from the rain soaking through (cold wet). If you wear wool under your weatherproof you will find that this will absorb the excess condensation without causing any discomfort.

On the feet should be worn a pair of knee-length loopstitch stockings, with another pair of loopstitch socks over them. Loopstitch is a special form of knitting which looks like towelling and completely covers the seams, thus making blistering much less likely. Two pairs of socks gives a pleasant cushioned effect and, as well-dubbined boots are practically impermeable, they will absorb a great deal of moisture given off by the feet. Most boots will let in a certain amount of moisture in really wet conditions but two pairs of socks will prevent any discomfort.

Modern walking boots usually have a sole made of hard moulded rubber with indentations based on the nailing pattern of old-fashioned boots to give maximum grip. (Moulded-rubber soles intended for industrial use are not suitable.) The uppers are soft leather, with a bellows tongue to prevent the ingress of water and hook-lacing for speed and maximum adjustment. Boots are likely to be the most expensive item of equipment purchased (£15–£25) and are difficult to choose because they need breaking in; ill-fitting boots can be crippling in a very few miles. Be sure to specify walking boots – climbing boots are not suitable as they have a metal plate inserted between the soles to give them stiffness. Take to the shop two pairs of walking socks to wear for the fitting. When fitted, there should be enough room to poke a forefinger behind the heel and the toes should just touch the boot at the front. This allows for the feet to swell when they get hot.

Boots need breaking in to make them conform to the shape of the feet and it can be some time before they are really comfortable. Firstly, they should be well dubbined, care being taken not to smear the grease onto the hard rubber soles. They should be worn about the house and in the garden, and then used for short walks. They will gradually become comfortable and soon be suitable for long walks. After each walk the boots should be cleaned. First gently scrape off the mud trapped in the interstices of the sole with a small blunt knife. Then, using a long-handled soft brush (a washing-up brush is ideal) and plenty of cold water, gently wash away all the mud. Stuff the boots with newspaper and leave for a few hours in a warm room well away from direct heat. When they are quite dry, they should be dubbined.

Weatherproof garments should be cleaned only with warm water, gently soaking off any mud. Woollen sweaters, shirts and socks should be washed by hand in soapflakes. Socks and stockings must have no darns in the foot as this is a sure recipe for blisters. Modern hose usually has nylon-reinforced heels and toes which give the socks a very long life.

Those who walk in lowland areas, especially if they intend to do some serious walking, will find the outfit described above will suit their needs very well, but none of it is essential. If you want to walk in canvas boots, or shoes, or wellington boots and carry a plastic mac then do so. You will come to no harm and your walking will cost you very little. In wet weather an indefatigable walking friend of mine wears a cloth cap, riding mac and wellington boots. It would not suit me but he is perfectly happy.

Other equipment likely to be required is a small rucksack for carrying spare items, a map case which allows the map to be protected yet read, first-aid kit, secateurs and a stick. Secateurs are useful for cutting back overgrown vegetation on stiles and a stick is invaluable for fending off inquisitive animals, testing the depth of mud and jumping over boggy patches. I never take either item in mountainous country, as there is no call for secateurs and a stick can be dangerous amongst rocks – it can easily trip the unwary. In mountainous country, a whistle should always be carried round the neck on a lanyard so that the international mountain distress signal can be given if the walker gets into difficulty. The signal is six blasts on the whistle repeated at minute intervals. A large plastic bag or space blanket should always be kept in the rucksack for use in mountainous country, as should a torch. A compass and pocket-knife complete the equipment.

Specialized equipment for use in the mountains in winter is described in Chapter 4.

Bibliography

BLACKSHAW, ALAN, *Mountaineering from Hill Walking to Alpine Climbing*, Penguin Books, 1975.

BOOTH, DERRICK, *The Backpacker's Handbook*, Hale, 1972.

LUMLEY, PETER, *Backpacking*, Teach Yourself Books, 1974.

LUMLEY, PETER, *Spur Book of Hill Trekking*, Spurbooks, 1977.

SPENCER, KATE, Compiler, *The Backpacker's Annual*, Continental Leisure Publications Ltd, 1977.

WILLIAMS, PETER F., *Camping and Hill Trekking*, Pelham Books, 1969.

Backpacking is the craft of carrying in a rucksack the essentials with which to support life for several days. Modern technology has produced reliable lightweight materials which ensure that the walker's load can be limited to about thirty pounds. He will be warm, comfortable and dry, and his evening meal can be prepared cleanly on a tiny stove in a few minutes. There is no need to be dirty, uncomfortable, wet or cold in order to enjoy the great outdoors, and cooking over an open fire is not only unpleasant but anti-social and contrary to the Country Code. Although the modern backpacker does not rough it, he does live much closer to nature than any other holidaymaker. There is a very special quality about a sunset seen from the door of a tent high up on a fellside, and only the most prosaic will not respond to the changing pattern of light in a mountain valley as the sun comes up. No food tastes better (even if it is dehydrated) than the meal cooked by a beck at the end of an exhilarating day's walking in the mountains.

Middle-aged walkers who remember the days of Commando rucksacks, when virtually the only camping equipment available was either war surplus or based upon designs used in the armed services, will marvel at modern equipment. Pup tents, mess tins, kapok-filled sleeping bags which resulted in the lightest pack weighing well over forty pounds seem prehistoric to the modern backpacker.

Weight is something to be considered very carefully when selecting equipment. It is possible to be too fanatical about saving ounces but it is surprising how quickly they can mount into pounds. It is perfectly possible, and indeed desirable, to ensure that the total weight of equipment does not exceed thirty pounds.

Rucksack

Modern rucksacks are usually made of totally waterproof polyurethane-coated nylon packs mounted on an aluminium frame. They are carried high on the back and are so designed that the weight is distributed down the body, so that the walker can walk in a natural posture without the need to lean forward to counterbalance the load. When using one of the old badly designed Commando-type rucksack with a heavy load, it was often necessary to lean so far forward that all the walker could see was his feet. The better rucksacks have a wide padded hip belt which is tightened after the pack is lifted onto the shoulders. The shoulder straps are then slackened and most of the weight is carried on the hips. It is quite astonishing how comfortable this type of rucksack can be, and I have often walked twenty-five miles in a day carrying a thirty-pound pack in mountainous country. The pack itself can be purchased in various styles to fit the frame chosen. Some packs consist of one main compartment with perhaps a couple of side pockets. Others have the main compartment divided into a number of sections into which can be packed a tent, sleeping bag, food and cooking equipment, clothes etc., and often as many as five side pockets. Whichever pack is chosen, the principle of packing the kit to be taken is the same. Light items go at the bottom and away from the frame, heavy items at the top and as close to the frame as possible.

A good pack frame and sac is likely to cost between £15 and £25.

Tent

Modern one-man tents for backpackers can be as light as $2\frac{1}{4}$ pounds. They are made of polyurethane-coated nylon, which is 100 per cent waterproof and will only let in water if damaged. But because the fabric is impermeable, there are problems of dampness inside the tent due to condensation. Various ingenious methods are employed to overcome condensation, including foam lining and permeable but waterproof inner tents which allow water vapour to pass through the inner tent, to condense on the underside of the impermeable skin. If water falls back on the inner tent, the silicone proofing will prevent it coming through and it will roll harmlessly down the edge of the tent where it can be shaken out before the tent is struck.

Some cheaper tents control condensation by means of ventilation. This is usually an acceptable method if cost is important, but there will inevitably be some dampness and it is advisable to have a small sponge handy to mop up the tiny pools of water. If the tent is properly designed, the walls will be angled so that the condensation rolls down the wall to the groundsheet rather than falling off onto the sleeping occupant! It is almost impossible to cook inside a single skin tent because of condensation problems and it is wise to select a tent with a porch under which to cook. All modern tents have sewn-in tray-shaped ground sheets.

Ultra-lightweight tents suitable for backpackers should not be used in high altitudes except in settled conditions in temperate weather. It is much better to seek the shelter of the valleys rather than try to ride out bad weather high in the mountains. Proper mountain tents designed to withstand gale-force winds in exposed places are much heavier than tents normally used by packpackers. A lightweight tent for backpacking will cost from £25–£60.

Sleeping Bags

The lightest and the most efficient sleeping bags are made of pure goose down, weigh just over two pounds and cost in the region of £60 plus.

Down sleeping bags are efficient because of the natural property of the filling which allows air to be trapped. This quality is known as 'loft' and is found to a lesser extent in other cheaper fillings allied to pure down, such as curled feathers. It is essential to preserve the quality of the loft by keeping the bag dry and unrolled except when it is in the rucksack. Before packing each day it should be aired.

Practically all down and feather sleeping bags are constructed on either the wall quilted or box principle. This method avoids the problems created by simple quilting as there is always a layer of insulation between the nylon inner lining and the outer cover which prevents cold spots (Figure 1).

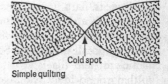

Box quilting Simple quilting

Fig. 1 Box quilting and simple quilting

Cheaper bags are filled with terylene, which is a good insulator but cannot compare with down except when damp. Terylene bags are approximately one-third of the cost of the best down bags and some of them weigh as little as $2\frac{1}{2}$ pounds. The best terylene bags are quite suitable for use anywhere in Britain during the summer months providing that an insulating mat is used and light woollen long johns, a sweater and woollen hat are worn. The resulting cash saving compared with down bags can be considerable. Sleeping bags come with and without zippers and they should be shaped so that they are wider at the shoulder and narrow at the foot and have a drawstring at the top so that they can be adjusted to fit snugly round the neck.

An insulating mat which goes under the floor of the tent should always be used with a sleeping bag. These are made of a non-porous closed-cell flexible material which completely insulates the sleeping bag from the ground thus preventing the loss of body heat, which could be considerable.

Insulating mats come in various sizes, but for summer use one measuring 38 ins. × 18 ins. is sufficient, as this will insulate the trunk leaving the legs and head hanging over the edge. Socks in a stuff bag make a suitable pillow and spare clothing can be used under the legs.

Cooking Equipment

Backpackers require the following qualities in a cooking stove. It must be light in weight, compact, efficient and clean, and fuel must be readily available. The most commonly used fuels are butane gas, solid fuel tablets, methylated spirits, paraffin and petrol. With any stove using liquid fuel there is a real risk of contaminating food. Methylated spirit and petrol are highly volatile, and petrol is difficult to obtain in small quantities. Solid fuel is very expensive and inefficient, and the heat cannot be controlled accurately. Bottled gas is widely available, easily handled and probably the safest fuel to use. With careful planning one 8-oz. container will last one person a week assuming that the stove is used only twice a day. The Vango S7000 stove is probably the most ingenious and lightest practical stove on the market for backpackers. It consists of a regulating tap which screws directly onto an 8-oz. Calor gas container and is then connected by a rubber tube to the burner. The whole stove measures 3½ ins. × 2½ ins. and weighs 6 oz., to which must be added 8 oz. for the fuel. It is clean and efficient and about the cheapest stove which can be regulated on the market. Stoves and fuel containers must always be left outside the tent at night to obviate the risk of lethal fumes leaking.

There are a number of compact light cooking pans which nest together. They usually have a frying pan, plate and saucepan, and with properly prepared menus this kit will be perfectly adequate. A polythene mug, a knife, fork and spoon set, which fit neatly together with a clip, an aluminium pot holder to remove saucepans from the stove, a tiny plastic condiment set, water-purifying tablets, non-safety matches individually sealed in candle wax against dampness and then kept in a 35-mm. film case with a piece of nail file on which to strike them, a small piece of green nylon scourer, and a minute baby can-opener complete the equipment.

Food and Menus

Backpackers require a balanced diet of a high calorific value with plenty of protein. All food should require the minimum of preparation and only a few minutes' cooking time. There is a wide variety of convenience food on the market which meet these requirements. A great deal of time can be saved if the food is packed into individual portions for each meal and the food for one day contained in a plastic bag. Consider a menu for one day; there is no need to cook breakfast as it can consist of a large plate of muesli (Alpen, Familia etc.) to which has been added sugar and dried milk to taste before the trip started. This individual portion can be poured from its plastic bag into a plate and water added. Fill the saucepan with water and put it on the stove. When the water boils, pour from a previously prepared tiny plastic bag a mixture containing a tea or coffee bag, dried milk and sugar. This makes a marvellous breakfast which will keep the walker going for two or three hours, and washing-up is kept to a minimum. Lunch consists of crispbread, cheese slices and dates or dried apricots. I have the same lunch every day and so have a special plastic bag kept at the top of my pack which contains all I need. Water is drunk straight from the container.

Dinner may consist of a can of meat heated in boiling water. Pour some dehydrated potato from an individual plastic bag into a plate and then add boiling water to make whipped potato mash. Remove the can of meat from the saucepan, and while keeping the water boiling pour in an individual portion of accelerated freeze dried peas which will cook in two minutes. Dessert can consist of dried fruit. Tea or coffee can be made before retiring for the night. Other dinner menus are a can of meat dropped into one of the quick cooking soups such as Chef or Batchelor's Cup of Soup. If a shop can be visited late in the afternoon it would be worth buying a can of Irish stew or some cooked meat and fresh fruit but it is not wise to carry heavy items like this very far. In my view, cooking should be kept as simple as possible, with a minimum of washing up. There are a number of firms, such as Springlow, specializing in lightweight foods suitable for backpackers, but unfortunately these are often expensive and available only from specialist shops far from the place they are to be eaten.

Personal Hygiene

No one likes to be dirty for long and at the end of a day's walking most of us are not nice to know at close quarters. A good wash at the end of the day can do wonders for morale and bestow a sense of well-being. On commercial camp sites, washing presents no problems, but it is more difficult if there are no wash basins available. It must be remembered that each person needs about four pints of water (weighing five pounds) to cover evening meal, breakfast and essential washing. If there is any doubt about the availability of water at a camp site, water must be obtained beforehand. There is usually no difficulty in finding water in mountainous country. It can be carried conveniently in a half-gallon plastic jerrycan in which supermarkets sell orange and lemon squash. Drinking water in lowland areas must be obtained only from a reliable household supply, but in the mountains and on the fells water from fast-running streams is usually fairly safe to drink, though water-purifying tablets available from a chemist's shop should be used.

A small washing-up bowl can be made by cutting off the top of a half-gallon round detergent container. This bowl is large enough to contain sufficient water for an elementary wash. Before retiring for the night, and whatever the weather, the backpacker must strip off and thoroughly sponge the body from head to foot, paying particular attention to the feet. Deodorants should not be used as it is unwise artificially to restrict sweating when exercising hard. Carry a small quantity of talcum powder, which will make you smell sweet and also be useful for powdering the feet.

I like to be clean-shaven and carry a battery-operated electric razor which I regard as my one luxury when backpacking, but perhaps many walkers would regard this practice with some derision!

A compact toothbrush which has a detachable handle into which the brush fits when not in use, toothpaste, flannel and towel and a partially used bar of soap carried in a freezer bag are all the toilet articles that are required.

Socks and underwear can be washed in the washing-up bowl. A small container of soap powder or mild detergent should be carried and this can also be used for washing-up. Clothes can be dried by hanging them from the back of the rucksack in dry weather, but as heavy woollen stockings take a long time to dry even in good weather they should be washed as soon as used.

Many backpackers find that they become constipated during the first few days of a walking holiday. Two or three Beechams pills carried in the first-aid box will be found useful and a small pack of tissues carried in the breast pocket will be found invaluable as handkerchiefs, tea towel and toilet tissue.

Proper sanitary arrangements must be made well away from any streams. Make a shallow pit about 3 ins. deep with a stick or the heel of your boot and then cover the stools with a thin layer of earth. Rubbish which will break down and rot may also be buried but tins and plastic bags should be disposed of properly in a litter bin even if this means carrying them a considerable distance; it is quite wrong to bury such articles.

Kit and Equipment

On the next page is listed my own backpacking outfit. I should like to own a more sophisticated tent and a down

	Weight	
	lb.	oz.
Camp Trails rucksack	3	4
Ultimate U8 tent	3	4
Black's Club sleeping bag	2	8
Karrimat		6
Vango S7000 stove		6
Butane cartridge		8
Canteen		15
Knife, fork and spoon		3
Panhandle		1
Cup		1
2-quart plastic water carrier		2
Washing-up bowl		1
Water-sterilizing tablets		$\frac{1}{2}$
Nylon scourer		$\frac{1}{2}$
Matches		1
2 pairs of long stockings	1	0
2 pairs of short oversocks		4
1 pair of pants		2
1 pair of cotton trousers		12
1 woollen shirt		15
1 pair of woollen long johns		8
Toilet kit		9
Towel (guest size)		6
Electric razor		9
Torch		4
1 pair of gaiters		8
1 pair of leggings		6
1 cagoule	1	8
Food for 3 days	5	0
Water	2	0
Survival bag		3
First-aid kit*		5
	27	00

Equipment not carried in the rucksack:
Clasp knife
Whistle
Silva compass
Map case

* See p. 222 for a description of what the kit should contain.

sleeping bag, but nevertheless these items have served me well and have proved to be a sound investment.

Camp Sites

Permission should normally be sought from the landowner before camping in open country. However, in some mountainous areas of Great Britain a tradition of tolerating *bona fide* backpackers has grown up, though notices forbidding camping must always be respected.

The essentials of a good camp site are a sheltered level spot, preferably on grass, and easy access to fresh water. Idyllic-looking sites near mountain streams should be viewed with caution as becks and ghylls can rise with surprising rapidity in heavy rain with the risk of flooding the tent. Choose a site into which rainwater will not drain and avoid areas where mist is likely to form.

The tent should be pitched with the entrance facing away from the prevailing wind. Many tents for backpackers are shaped so that the occupants have to sleep with their heads near the door, so unless the ground is level it is important that the site should slope gently away to the feet. Having selected the site, remove any stones and hassocks of grass so that there are no bumps underneath the floor of the tent.

Wet clothes, boots, rucksacks and cooking equipment should be kept in the porch of the tent. If your tent lacks a porch, store these items in a large plastic bag weighted with stones outside the tent. Camping is much more pleasurable if everything is kept scrupulously clean and tidy and has its allotted place in the tent. This will help the backpacker to strike camp and make an early start. Before leaving the site look round carefully to ensure that you have left no trace of your passing.

Bibliography

ADSHEAD, ROBIN, *Backpacking in Britain*, Oxford Illustrated Press, 1974.

ADSHEAD, ROBIN, *Spur Book of Basic Backpacking*, Spurbooks, 1977.

BOOTH, DERRICK, *The Backpacker's Handbook*, Hale, 1972.

COX, JACK, *Lightweight Camping; A Practical Guide for Projects and Expeditions in Britain and Europe*, Lutterworth Press, 1972.

LUMLEY, PETER, *Backpacking*, Teach Yourself Books, 1974.

SPENCER, KATE, Compiler, *The Backpacker's Annual*, Continental Leisure Publications Ltd, 1977.

WILLIAMS, PETER, *Beginner's Guide to Lightweight Camping*, Pelham Books, 1975.

WILLIAMS, PETER, *Camping Complete*, Pelham Books, 1972.

WILLIAMS, PETER, *Camping and Hill Trekking*, Pelham Books, 1969.

WALKING
TECHNIQUES

The serious walker knows that there is a good deal more to walking than being able to put one foot in front of the other. Technique is unimportant to the ambler who is content to do five or six miles, but the person who enjoys a fifteen, twenty or twenty-five mile tramp, especially if it is repeated day after day, as it would be on a walking holiday, will tend to develop his own style and subconsciously learn the techniques of good walking. If the neophyte is aware of the techniques before he starts walking seriously, he will learn more quickly.

Great physical strength is not necessary but stamina is important. I am below average height, am slightly built and weigh under ten stone yet I have often walked twenty-five miles in a day; the furthest I have walked in one day is thirty-two miles and the hardest day's walking of my life was the last stage of the Pennine Way when, carrying a thirty-pound pack, I walked the twenty-seven miles in driving rain and gale-force winds, sinking up to my knees at times in peat bogs.

On level ground use your natural stride and resist any temptation to lengthen it. On a gradient the stride should be shortened but the legs should move at the same speed, maintaining the rhythm of walking. Perhaps the best analogy is that of a motor car driven by an engine maintaining a constant speed, with the road speed controlled by infinitely variable gearing. When the hill is exceptionally steep, some walkers find it worthwhile to adopt a zig-zag route, moving one or two steps at an angle of 45° to the slope and then 45°

in the opposite direction, rather like a yacht sailing against the wind. This makes the route longer but less arduous.

Whenever possible, put the whole of the sole of the foot down on firm ground and avoid toe and heel holds. The experienced walker always chooses the easiest route along an uneven path and rarely stumbles or loses his balance. If one route on a path becomes unwalkable, retrace a few steps and seek an alternative, as this is much less tiring and dangerous than jumping down or scrambling up. It is very dangerous to jump even from small heights with a heavy pack – the weight can easily unbalance the unwary and can cause compression fractures and spinal injury.

The novice may be surprised to learn that it is usually more tiring to descend a steep hill than to climb it, especially with a heavy pack. A long descent puts great strain on the muscles at the front of the thighs and unless the walker is fit these muscles can become very tender. The secret of walking down steep hills is to allow the legs to bend slightly at the knee so that the body is not jarred when each foot is put on the ground. If the ground is not too rough it is a good plan to run downhill in a skipping motion taking very short steps and turning 45° every few yards. In one or two places on steep and rocky paths it may be helpful to turn round and come down backwards, especially with a heavy pack.

It is important to conserve energy as much as possible and to avoid unnecessary exertion. Therefore, do not swing the arms in an exaggerated fashion as do soldiers on a route march. The arms can help the walker to maintain his balance, but an expert walker will be quite happy to clasp his hands behind his back or lightly grasp the bottom of his rucksack while walking on level, even ground.

When setting out on a long walk, start off slowly, well within your normal walking pace, and gradually work up to your usual speed and stride. This is particularly important in mountainous country, when the walk usually starts from the valley with a long climb. It is a sure sign of the novice to rush up the first hill, sink down at the top to regain his breath and then gallop down the other side. The experienced walker will climb up slowly, perhaps pause for a minute at the top to admire the view and regain breath and then continue steadily and rhythmically down the other side, soon leaving our novice far behind.

Speed and Distance

Sooner or later, the inevitable question of how far to walk arises. The only reasonable answer is: as far as you want and are able. Most fell-walkers will find that fifteen miles is as much as they want to do in a day. The distance is sufficient to have covered a reasonable amount of country and experience a variety of scenery, but it cannot be emphasized too much that the distance covered is unimportant. A pleasant afternoon stroll of five miles or so on a sunny day can be infinitely more pleasant and rewarding than 'bog-trotting' for twenty miles in driving rain when the mist and the rain blot out the scenery. Although fell-walking is generally regarded as more strenuous than walking through the fields and woods of lowland country it is not necessarily so. In mountainous areas, the path is usually well-defined and, except in boggy patches, the surface is firm, whereas paths in cultivated areas are often ploughed or ill-defined and the natural rhythm of walking is broken by the need to climb stiles, to open gates and to examine the map at every field boundary.

It is important to be able to calculate the length of time a walk will take. This information is often required in order to catch a train or a bus, or rendezvous with a car at a suitable pick-up point, or to avoid being caught out after dark on a winter's afternoon. It is generally believed that a good average walking pace is three miles per hour. This is probably true on roads, but there are not many walkers who can average three miles per hour, excluding meal breaks, on paths. The most generally accepted method of calculating the time necessary to complete a walk in mountainous country is by Naismith's rule or formula, which states: 'allow one hour for every three miles measured on the map, plus an additional hour for every 2,000 ft climbed'. The distance climbed is not the highest point reached but the sum total of all the ascents. For instance, in Figure 2 the total height climbed is 2,900 ft, for which 1½ hours should be

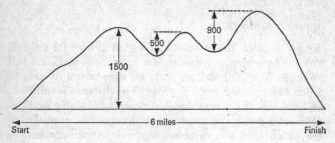

Fig. 2 Naismith's formula

allowed, the distance walked is 6 miles, for which 2 hours is allowed, and the total walking time is therefore 3½ hours. This formula assumes good conditions. Extra time should be allowed for bad weather, difficulties in route-finding, heavy packs and meal stops. Remember, too, that a party tends to be slower than an individual because time is wasted at difficult points along the route and the whole party never needs to go to the loo at the same time.

In lowland country, intensively farmed, allow two miles per hour plus time for meal stops. A large party is likely to take considerably longer because of the extra time taken to climb stiles and negotiate ploughed fields. Probably the fastest walking is on chalk downs, where there are few stiles or gates, where the paths tend to be well marked and the turf is gloriously springy underfoot. In such conditions, an average of three miles per hour walking time may be maintained.

Assuming that one has the stamina, the secret of walking long distances – say twenty miles and more – is not so much walking fast as to keep going with a minimum of stops. Study the map carefully beforehand and memorize the route, making a note of any difficulties. Train yourself to walk for three or four hours at a stretch without stops except perhaps for two or three minutes at the summit of a stiff climb. When you do stop for a meal and rest, choose a comfortable spot out of the wind, take off your boots and rucksack and after eating and drinking lie flat on your back for fifteen minutes and relax completely. Any slight stiffness in the thigh muscles and joints will disappear a few minutes after starting to walk again. Be prepared to shorten your route or go back if the weather turns bad. Do not overlook the psychology of the early start, for every hour of walking before lunchtime is worth two of those after lunch. A walk which seems hard if started after nine in the morning can be easy if begun at seven o'clock, and dawn is the most witching hour of the day.

Path Surfaces

The soil which forms the surface of a path has certain qualities and it is as well to know the different characteristics of each type as they affect the walker. It is assumed that hard moulded-rubber soles are worn.

ROCK   Dry rock of all kinds, from sandstone to granite, provides a good surface on which the boots will not slip. Rubber soles grip reasonably well on clean (i.e. lichen- or mud-free) rock but when rock is covered with lichen or mud (usually known as greasy rock) great care is necessary as it is easy to slip. Ice-covered rock is lethal.

SCREE   Scree is loose pieces of rock, about the size of large pebbles, on a steep mountain slope. It is very fatiguing to climb because when advancing one step you slip back half a step, rather like climbing steep shingle on the beach. However, scree can be fun to descend. Run down the slope boldly, digging in the heels at each step. The loose rock will move under your feet, as shingle would, but it is very bad for the boots.

PEAT   Peat is formed by decomposing vegetation, usually heather and bracken, and is a dark chocolate colour. Dry

peat provides a good surface, pleasantly springy underfoot. Wet peat is slightly slippery, but as it tends to be
covered with heather it causes difficulties only when deep
and free from vegetation. In wet weather on some fells,
especially Kinder Scout in the Peak District, it is possible
to sink to one's knees in peat bogs. With a little experience
it is possible to see firmer footing provided by clumps of
sphagnum grass and bog cotton which will help to keep
you from sinking too deeply into the bog.

GRASS Grass provides pleasant walking though it is slippery on slopes when wet.

CLAY Clay is dreadful stuff. If frozen or baked hard, it
becomes rutted and one fears for one's ankles at every
step. When waterlogged, it is as slippery as a skating rink.
Clay, when ploughed, clings tenaciously to the boots in
great lumps, increasing the weight on the feet several-
fold. It is very difficult to remove, but the worst can be
got off with the aid of a stick and plenty of thick wet grass.
It is often helpful to kick an imaginary football as this will
loosen the largest lumps.

CHALK The finest and most springy turf grows on chalk.
With heavy use the grass is worn away exposing the chalk
which can then erode badly. This happens frequently at
the most popular beauty spots in the chalk country of
southern England. It provides a good firm surface when
dry, although it marks the boots distinctively, but it is
treacherous when wet as it becomes very slippery. Wet
escarpments should be avoided whenever possible.

SAND Sandy soils always drain exceptionally well and are
pleasant to walk on in all weathers.

Stiles and footbridges are often very slippery when wet
and great care must be taken when negotiating them.

Fell-Walking in Winter

After the walker has gained some experience, he may wish
to venture onto the fells in winter. Even though there may

be no snow about, the conditions on the tops are likely to be arctic, with very cold winds, and it is absolutely essential to go properly dressed and equipped. Wear windproof clothing in the form of anorak, cagoule or fell-jacket and overtrousers together with extra woollen sweaters and woollen long johns. Head and hands should be protected with a balaclava helmet or woollen hat which will cover the ears and woollen gloves or mitts with windproof over-mitts in the severest weather. It is much better and warmer to wear layers of thin woollen clothing rather than one heavy sweater. Down clothing is excellent but expensive. It is essential only in the extreme conditions which may be encountered in the north of Scotland. Carry a rucksack large enough to contain all the spare clothing, take plenty of food and a hot drink, a survival bag and first-aid kit. Do not go alone, and leave word of your route with someone responsible, not forgetting to report your safe return. Be sure to check the local weather forecast before setting off and do not go if bad conditions are expected.

If snow is lying on the ground, special precautions and equipment are necessary. Snow makes even familiar paths and routes look different and often obscures cairns and other features useful for route-finding. There are many varieties of snow, depending on the weather conditions. Fresh snow is the easiest and safest to negotiate but it can be very annoying if more than ankle-deep. Snow that has been lying some time is likely to have been subjected to alternate freezing and thawing which puts a crust on it which makes for much firmer footholds. If the snow lasts long enough the constant thawing and freezing will make it very hard or perhaps turn it into ice. Rocks are likely to be covered in ice crystals and streams will be surrounded by large areas of ice.

Rubber soles do not give a good grip on hard snow and ice, so crampons must be worn. The best crampons are 'lobster claws' and consist of ten or twelve spikes on a frame which is strapped to the soles of the boots (Figure 3). There are two forward-projecting spikes which are extremely useful for kicking steps in encrusted snow. Crampons have to be

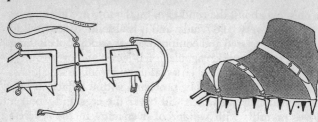

Fig. 3 Lobster-claw crampons

adjusted so that they fit the boot tightly and this will probably entail bending the frame slightly so that when pressed
into position without the bindings attached they will not
drop off when the boot is shaken. Care must be taken when
handling crampons as they can tear stockings and inflict
lacerations if the wearer stumbles. With ordinary crampons
(ones without the front lobster claw) it is necessary to walk
with all the points in contact with the snow, and on a slope
this can be cumbersome and uncomfortable. With lobster-
claw crampons, it is possible to walk up slopes using only the
front four points, which makes for easier and speedier progress.

If conditions warrant the wearing of crampons, an ice axe
(Figure 4) should be carried for step-cutting in ice. An ice
axe has a head consisting of an edge for cutting steps in hard
snow and brittle ice and a pick for use on hard ice. The
handle is wood or metal with a metal spike in the end which

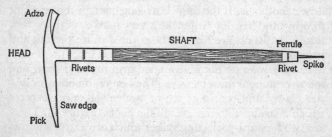

Fig. 4 Ice axe

can be used for belaying. Handles come in various lengths
and it is important to choose one that matches your height.
The correct length can be determined by holding the axe by
the handle with the head downwards. The tip of the spike
should be about one inch off the ground. Ice axes should be
carried with the spike pointing forwards and downwards.
When not likely to be required, the axe can be attached head
upwards to the shoulder straps of the rucksack or inside the
rucksack with the handle resting on the bottom of the pack.
It is advisable to cover the spike to prevent damage.

All fell-walkers who venture out in snowy conditions
should know how to use an ice axe as a brake in the event of
a fall on snow-covered slopes (Figure 5). It is wise to practise

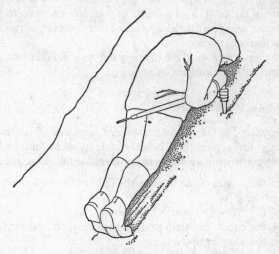

Fig. 5 Braking with an ice axe

the technique on a safe slope until you can do it properly
every time. As soon as you start to fall, roll over onto your
chest keeping your feet up so that your crampons do not
catch in the snow and cause you to somersault. Get the shaft
of your ice axe under your armpit and, leaning on the head,
force the pick end into the snow. If done properly, it will

W.H.—3

effectively bring you to a stop on slopes up to an angle of 40°.

Ice axes can also be used for cutting steps if the surface is too hard for steps to be kicked. Hold the axe with both hands on the spike end of the handle and allow the weight of the axe to drive it into the snow and through the ice. With practice it should be possible to learn to cut a step in two or three blows, because the fewer blows struck, the quicker will be the progress and the minimum possible amount of energy will be expended.

On steep ascents, where the walker intends to take the most direct route, the steps should point inwards to the slope and they should be cut so that the sole of the boot can be accommodated. When descending steep slopes, traversing a slope or zig-zagging, long flat steps should be cut to take the whole of the boot. You should cut your steps nearest to you and then work further away so that you can take advantage of the first cut made.

I cannot emphasize too strongly that you should be taught ice and snow techniques by an expert.

Leading Walks

Experienced walkers are sometimes approached by rambling clubs, schools and local organizations to lead walks. Before consenting, it is wise to agree on the following points:

(a) the length of the walk in the light of the experience of those taking part;
(b) the type of terrain to be covered;
(c) the conditions under which you are prepared to lead;
(d) the number in the party.

It is absolutely essential for the leader to survey the walk a month or so before it takes place. Make a note of any particular problems such as missing footbridges, overgrown stiles etc., and take steps to see that the more serious matters are rectified before the walk takes place or an alternative route will have to be arranged. A tactful letter or phone call to a farmer telling him you are leading a walk will often get a stile put in across a barbed-wire fence. County Councils have been known to erect footbridges speedily and they are worth approaching, but unless the stream is very wide and deep a little ingenuity can often overcome the problem. For example, if a stream has to be forded it may well be possible to get reasonably close to the point by car and take a couple of breeze blocks to the ford before the walk takes place.

Having satisfied yourself that the route is practicable, issue instructions, if necessary, on the type of clothes and footwear to be worn together with details of food and drink to be taken and the time the walk will take, keeping in mind that a large party will move much more slowly than a small group. When the walk starts, designate someone to be the gate shutter and to bring up the rear so that the party does not straggle too much. Before moving off, it is a good plan to mention briefly the need to obey the Country Code and, in particular, to walk through growing crops in single file.

Even with the most careful preparations, things can go wrong. I was once walking with two Girl Guides training for their Duke of Edinburgh Award expedition test. As we entered one field, a herd of heifers at the far end came galloping towards us. The girls were nervous, but I assured them that the cattle would stop in plenty of time and, to prove the point, I waved my stick at them and found myself face to face with a bull, who was clearly very put out at my cavalier treatment of his harem. I told the girls to move cautiously to the gate and out of the corner of my eye saw them climb it. I then backed slowly to the gate and quickly vaulted over it. My sudden movement upset the bull and he began swinging his head angrily. Imagine my horror when I saw that in her nervousness one of the girls had slipped on the gate and was hanging helplessly through the bars with her head only a few inches from the bull. I had to drag her clear in a none too gentle fashion and it was several minutes before she had recovered sufficiently to continue the walk.

Another incident was more amusing but caused no little discomfort. I was leading a walk during a very wet spring when most of the fields were waterlogged. One gateway was especially muddy and churned up by cattle and a lady lost her wellington boot. All our efforts to find it failed and the men took it in turns to give her a piggy back to the nearest road.

Leading walks in the mountains and on the fells is a much more serious business. It is essential for the leader to insist on every member of the party being properly dressed and equipped with foul-weather gear, large plastic bag and food and drink (including an emergency supply). The leader should have an inspection before moving off and refuse to take anyone without the necessary kit and equipment. It is generally accepted that one leader should not be in charge of more than ten walkers and so, for a large party, several leaders may be required. It is much better for each group of ten to move off separately rather than attempt to keep together. Each leader must have a first-aid kit and a list of names and addresses and telephone numbers of everyone in his party. Details of the route and estimated time of arrival must be left with a responsible person.

In view of some of the appalling accidents that have happened in recent years to school parties in the mountains, education authorities now insist that leaders of groups of people venturing into the mountains must possess a Mountain Leadership Certificate (see p. 251). There is much argument among mountaineers about the value of these qualifications, but although it is true that many walkers not possessing the MLC may well have better experience and judgement than some that have passed the examination it does provide some kind of standard on which a leader can be judged.

The United Kingdom is probably the best-mapped country
in the world. The Ordnance Survey was first established
after it was discovered that royal troops were at a great disadvantage during the Jacobite uprising because of a lack of
accurate maps. When peace was established, it was decided
to map the whole of the country at a scale of 1 in. to the mile.
The first map was published in 1801 and the Ordnance Survey has been busily mapping ever since. The maps range in
scale from 1:63360 (the famous 1 in. to the mile with which
most walkers are familiar, which have now been replaced by
the 1:50000) to 1:1250 or 50 ins. to the mile. In practice,
walkers are likely to use the 1 in., the 1:50000 (1¼ ins. to the
mile) and the 1:25000 (2½ ins. to the mile), although occasionally it may be useful to consult the larger-scale maps
for particular purposes. The Ordnance Survey also publish
special maps such as historical and geological maps which
can be useful and interesting to those pursuing a particular
hobby. Keen map-users can obtain free from the Ordnance
Survey, Maybush, Southampton, a copy of their current
map catalogue.

In one brief chapter it is quite impossible to give an
adequate description of the riches contained in Ordnance
Survey maps. They are wonderful mines of information,
works of art in themselves, and repay careful study. It is a
salutary experience to sit down for a couple of hours with
one of these maps and make a study of the key and then
relate it to the map.

Most walkers are familiar with the *folded* Ordnance Survey maps which come complete with a cover. However, many people prefer to buy the flat *unfolded* versions as they are cheaper and can be cut or folded to fit map cases. If a lot of walking is done in one particular area, it is a good plan to buy two copies of the required map and to cut each one in a different way so that each section of one map overlaps a section of the other. If two sections are placed back to back in a transparent map case a wide area of country will be covered and, when the edge of one map is reached, by turning over the map case your position on the second map will be some way from the edge of the map. This is a great advantage when route-finding.

Certain considerations have to be borne in mind when using any of the Ordnance Survey maps. Pay particular attention to the date of the survey, which will be found somewhere on the map, for a map can only be accurate at the time of the survey. The countryside is constantly if only imperceptibly changing; new roads are built, old roads are re-aligned, canals are filled in and reservoirs created, building development takes place, farmers grub hedges and erect new barns and woods are felled and forests planted. The map-user must always think of the possible changes which may have happened since the date of the survey, especially if the map apparently does not agree with the terrain!

The reputation of the Ordnance Survey is such that many people believe all their maps to be absolutely accurate. A little reflection will show that this cannot be the case because the scale itself prevents it. For example, on the 1:50000 map, unclassified roads with a minimum width of 4·3 metres are represented by a yellow line 1 millimetre wide. Yet strictly speaking 1 millimetre represents 50 metres on the ground on a map of this scale. If the roads were drawn exactly to scale they would be almost invisible.

The National Grid

All Ordnance Survey maps with a minimum scale of 1 in. to the mile show the full national grid. Each map has been divided into squares with the lines running almost exactly due north to south and east to west. The grid lines are spaced at kilometre intervals and are used for providing an exact reference to any given point on any edition of the map, and for compass work, described later in this chapter. To give a full grid reference:

(1) Establish from the map the letters which designate the 100-km. square in which the map falls, SP in Figure 6.

(2) Find the km. square which contains the feature to which you wish to assign a grid reference.

(3) Identify the horizontal grid line immediately south of the feature.

(4) From the *western* edge of the map follow this line until you meet the vertical grid line immediately to the *west* of the feature.

(5) Follow this vertical grid line to the bottom of the map where a number will be found. This should be written down.

(6) Follow the grid line back to near the feature and esti-mate the number of tenths of a grid square along the hori-zontal line the feature lies, and write down this number.

(7) You now have half of your grid reference known as an easting. Repeat the process on a vertical plane to establish your northing and you will end up with a six-figure refer-ence which occurs only once in every 100 km. If the letters for the 100-km. square are used, the reference is unique. The reference for the point in Figure 6, for example, is SP 138235.

Always find your eastings before your northings and re-member it by imagining the squirrel which runs along the grass and then up the tree There is an excellent explanation of the national grid on most copies of Ordnance Survey maps.

Grid references are invaluable for establishing meeting places. It is much better to agree to meet at SP 707212 than at 'the gate on the right-hand side of the road about a quarter of a mile beyond the railway bridges on the Quain-ton to Edgcott Lane'.

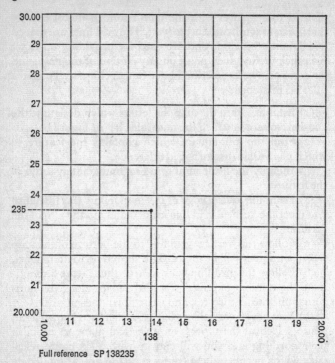

Full reference SP 138235

Fig. 6 Grid references

The 1:63360 Map (1 in. to the mile)

This map is the one with which most people are familiar. Each sheet covers an area of approximately 700 square miles. As part of the general conversion to metric standards, the 1-in. map has now been superseded by the 1:50000 map described below, which has a scale of approximately 1¼ ins. to the mile.

Some of the more popular walking areas of the country have had Tourist editions of the 1-in. map produced and these will continue to be available even though the 1-in. series as a whole is obsolete. The maps cover a much larger area but are otherwise similar to the normal 1-in. maps. Tourist maps are available for:

North York Moors
Loch Lomond and the Trossachs
New Forest
Peak District
Lake District
Exmoor
Dartmoor
Ben Nevis and Glen Coe
Cairngorms

This series of maps is quite suitable for walking in the wilder parts of the country on moors and mountains where land is largely uncultivated, except for forestry, and where the most significant natural features are likely to be hills and streams. I have used them extensively in the Pennines and in the Lake District without referring to larger-scale maps. However, even the most skilful map-reader will be unable to follow the exact line of the path in intensively farmed areas, where the most significant feature for identifying the line of the path is the field boundary, which is not shown on the 1-in. maps. These maps, nevertheless, are invaluable for planning walks. They show rights of way, distinguishing between footpaths and bridleways, and they have the advantage over the larger-scale maps in that they are revised quite regularly and are clear and easy to use.

1:50000 Maps (2 cm. to the km. or approximately 1¼ ins. to the mile)

These maps have superseded the 1-in. map and are totally metric except that the interval between contour lines is 50 ft, although every marked contour is given in metres. They have been compiled from photographically enlarged copies of the seventh series of the 1-in. map. When the second series is published, it will be based upon a new survey. Information about the state of revision is given on each map and should be noted carefully. Although slightly larger in scale than the 1-in. map, this new series does not give quite the same amount of detail. For example, no distinction is now made between coniferous and deciduous woods. Rights of way information is included, but these maps have been criticized because the red dotted lines for footpaths are difficult to follow among the orange contour lines. Like the 1-in. map, this map is uitable for use in high uncultivated areas but has limited use in lowland areas except for route-planning.

1:25000 First Series (4 cm. to the km. or approximately $2\frac{1}{2}$ ins. to the mile)

These are superb maps, showing the countryside in great detail and are essential for walking in lowland pastoral areas. They are available for the whole country except for the Highlands and the islands of Scotland. Each sheet covers an area of 100 sq. km., although some of the sheets covering coastal areas are larger. All these maps have been partially revised since the war, but as they are gradually being replaced by the Second Series (see below) no major revision will take place, except that, when any map is reprinted, important changes such as motorways and reservoirs will be added. The most important feature shown for walkers in lowland areas is the field boundary, be it a hedge, a wall or a fence. This enables the walker to follow the true line of the path with great confidence and to recognize immediately the field he is in. No distinction is made between private and public paths nor between footpaths and bridleways, so before they can be used with certainty they must be compared with the smaller-scale Ordnance Survey maps or, better still, the County Council's official rights-of-way map, and the public paths distinctively marked.

There is a simple method of determining the 1:25000 maps required for a given area from the appropriate 1:63360 or 1:50000 map. Each bold 10-km. grid line delineates the area covered by one map in the 1:25000 First Series. Somewhere on the map will be found a statement of the incidence of grid letters and numbers. Write down the grid letters found and then turn to the 10-km. square in which you are interested. Write down the first bold letter in the north–south grid on the western side then the kilometre grid square. Next, write down the first bold letter on the southern side of the east–west grid of the 10-km. grid square. This will give you the sheet number required. For example:

Incidence of grid letters: S P
First bold letter of the western side of the north–south grid: 8
First bold letter of southern side of east–west grid: 2
Therefore the sheet number required: S P 82

Outdoor Leisure Maps

These are the 1:25000 version of the 1-in. Tourist maps. They cover a much greater area than the normal 1:25000 sheets and include information about rights of way, boundaries of access land, access points, access paths, National Trust land, mountain rescue posts, youth hostels, camping and caravan sites.

Outdoor Leisure maps exist for the following areas:

The Dark Peak (Kinder Scout, Bleaklow and Black Hill)
The Three Peaks (Whernside, Ingleborough and Pen-y-Ghent)
The English Lakes (a set of four maps)
High Tops of the Cairngorms
Brighton and Sussex Vale
Cuillin and Torridon Hills
Malham and Wharfedale
The Brecon Beacons (a set of three maps)
The Wye Valley and Forest of Dean

1:25000 (Second Series)

These are probably the most beautiful maps produced in this country and are a joy to use. Unfortunately, not many are yet available and it will be 1990 before the whole country is covered. Each map covers an area twice the size of the First Series, measuring 20 km. by 10 km., using the same numbering system as the First Series, though each map is given two numbers to coincide with the appropriate two sheets of the First Series, for instance SS 43/53. Field boundaries are shown, as are rights of way if the information was available when the sheet was prepared.

The 1:25000 Second Series map required can be determined from the 1:63360 or 1:50000 map in exactly the same way as described for the First Series above. Each sheet of the Second Series covers twice the area of the First Series, so that this method will give you only half of the sheet number, but this will be enough to identify the map required.

Other Maps

Two other maps are useful for occasional reference. The 6 ins. to the mile (1:10580), now gradually being replaced by the 1:10000 (approximately 6½ ins. to the mile), can be very useful for establishing the true line of the path where it is not entirely clear on the smaller-scale maps. The 25 ins. to the mile map (1:2500) gives Ordnance Survey field numbers which are often referred to in planning applications and proposals for diverting and extinguishing paths. Large public libraries, estate agents and surveyors usually have these maps for their area.

Map-Reading

A map gives a representation of the area it covers by using symbols. In order to understand and use the map properly it is necessary to be able to interpret the symbols used, which will be found in the key somewhere on the map. These symbols vary slightly depending on the scale and series map being used. The most common can be quickly learned, but do be aware that some symbols have variants which, in some cases, can provide vital information, especially if you are

lost. For example, there are three symbols used on the
1:50000, 1:63360 and 1:25000 maps to indicate churches
and chapels:

   ⛪ church or chapel with tower
   ⛪ church or chapel with spire
   + church or chapel without either

This means that it may be possible to identify a village
from a hillside by the kind of church it has. Note that some
symbols look very similar. On the 1:50000 map these very
similar symbols are used to delineate different things and it
is necessary to check the key constantly until the map reader
is thoroughly familiar with all the symbols. For example:

        + church or chapel without spire
        + site of antiquity
  − + − + − National boundary

The feature on Ordnance Survey maps which is most confusing and difficult for beginners to grasp is the system of
indicating heights by contours. Once understood, it is possible to visualize the shape of the land from the configuration
of the contour lines (Figure 7). Perhaps the easiest way of
describing how contour lines indicate height is to imagine
the surveyor slicing the top off each hill and continuing to
carve it at regular intervals. Thus each contour line represents the circumference of one slice. It is obvious that the
closer the contour lines the steeper the slope. Conversely, a
walker who followed a contour line accurately would remain at exactly the same height.

There are no two hills in the country with exactly the
same contour lines, but physical features do fall into certain
easily recognizable categories which it is helpful to be able
to recognize.

The Silva Compass

The compass is an essential accompaniment of a map. In
order to get the maximum from a map, it is vital to know

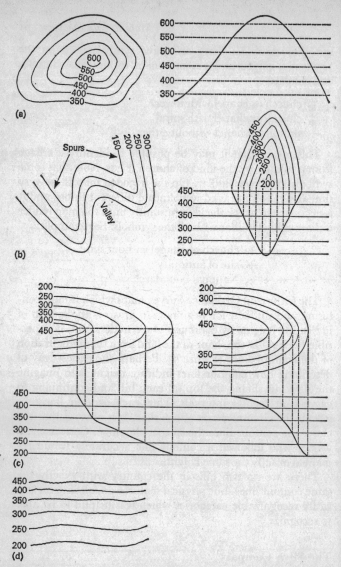

Fig. 7 Contours: (a) hill; (b) valley; (c) concave and convex slopes; (d) escarpment

how to use a compass accurately. It is very unwise to venture onto moors or mountains without a compass as it is invaluable for route-finding in mist. Even in lowland country, a compass is useful – it can be used for pinpointing stiles and gates on the route of paths. I have walked at night on paths I have never used before by taking compass bearings at each field boundary.

The best compass for walkers is an orienteering compass made by the Silva company. There are various models but they all have the same essential features. The type 4S illustrated in Figure 8 is typical. The compass is mounted in a

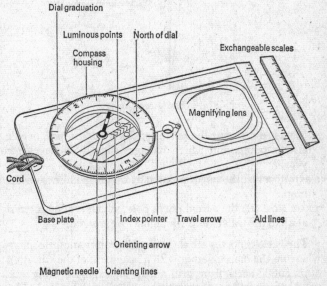

Fig. 8 Silva compass type 4S

transparent perspex base containing a small magnifying glass. On the base of the compass housing is engraved an arrow which points to the north on the edge of the housing. Parallel to the arrow are engraved lines. The whole of the compass housing can turn on the perspex base.

Before using a compass, it is necessary to grasp certain fundamental principles. On every Ordnance Survey map three norths are shown (see Figure 9):

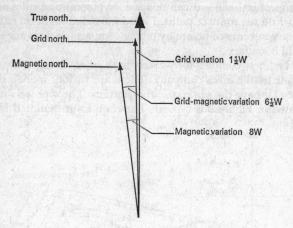

Fig. 9 The three norths

MAGNETIC NORTH: the north to which the compass needle always points and which changes slightly from year to year.

GRID NORTH: the north pointed at by the grid lines on the map.

TRUE NORTH: the actual north pole, which is of no interest at all to the walker and which may be ignored.

The various norths are shown in diagrammatic form somewhere on the map together with a statement of the variation of magnetic north from grid north; for example 'Magnetic north about $8\frac{1}{2}°$ west of grid north in 1974 decreasing by about $\frac{1}{2}°$ in eight years'.

The Silva compass can be used in a number of ways, each one of which should be mastered by practising the techniques in familiar surroundings before venturing into unknown territory where your very life may depend upon its accurate use.

A. How to Stay on Course (Figure 10): Let us suppose you are on a fell following an indistinct path. You know your position on the map and your destination is a mountain peak you can see some miles ahead of you. You notice some low cloud

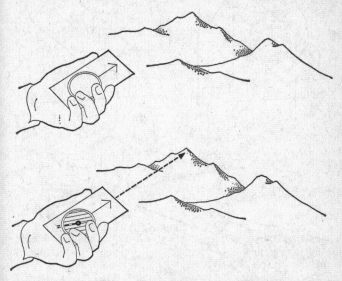

Fig. 10 How to stay on course

coming down which will obscure your destination. Take your compass and point the direction-of-travel arrow at the peak you wish to reach. Turn the compass housing until the arrow on the base of the housing points in the same direction as the north (red) end of the compass needle. Keep the compass needle and the arrow on the base of the housing in line and follow the direction-of-travel arrow. Rather than keeping the eye glued to the direction-of-travel arrow it is easier and more accurate to find an object such as a cairn, tree or boulder on the line of the path somewhere near the limit of visibility and walk towards it repeating the process until the destination is reached.

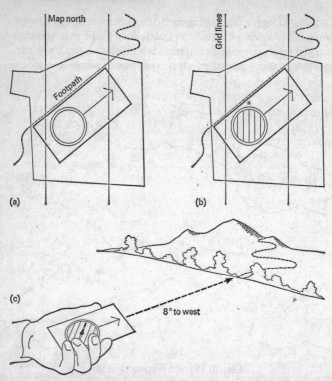

Fig. 11 Plotting a course

B. Plotting a Course from the Map (Figure 11): Very often paths follow straight lines between well-defined features. A path rarely curves across a field and even in mountainous country they are often straight unless following a natural feature such as a stream.

Using an Ordnance Survey map and a Silva compass it is possible to plot your course beforehand by noting down the compass bearing at each point the path changes direction. The method is as follows:

(1) Place the map on a flat surface. It is *not* necessary to

orientate it (i.e. position it so that the northern edge faces north).

(2) Place the straight perspex base of the compass along the line of the path to be followed (Figure 11a).

(3) Without moving the base, turn the compass housing until the arrow points towards the north end of the map and is exactly parallel to the north–south grid lines (Figure 11b).

(4) In order to get the arrow in the compass housing to point to grid north it is necessary to ADD the magnetic variation found at the bottom of the map by moving the compass housing the appropriate number of degrees.

(5) Read off the bearing from the point indicated on compass and note it down. When reaching that point in the walk set the compass for that bearing and, holding it in your hand, turn your body until the red arrow in the compass housing is in line with the north-pointing needle.

(6) The line of the path runs where the direction-of-travel arrow on the base plate of the compass is pointing (see Figure 11).

The above method illustrates the principles of using the Silva compass and the relationship between grid north and magnetic north. Once these principles are grasped, it is possible to make a short cut in the method. Instead of adding the magnetic variation (usually 8°) to the grid bearing, point the compass needle to 352° instead of 360° or magnetic north (see Figure 12). Many walkers stick a strip of sticky paper to the underside of the compass to mark the difference between grid north and magnetic north.

The method of plotting a course now becomes:

(1) Place the straight edge of the base along the line of the path.

(2) Without moving the base, turn the compass housing so that the arrow in the housing points towards the north end of the map and exactly parallel to the north–south grid lines.

(3) Remove compass from the map and holding the compass in front of you turn your body until the north end of the

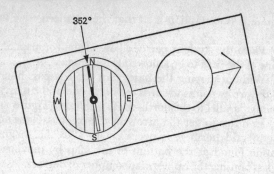

Fig. 12 Correcting for magnetic variation

compass needle points to 352° (or the appropriate magnetic variation, as it varies slightly in different parts of the country).

(4) The line of the path runs where the direction-of-travel arrow is pointing.

C. Finding Your Exact Position on the Map (Figure 13): Very often you may be walking along a path and although you are not lost you wish to know your precise position on that path. Your position can be found as follows:

(1) Select a prominent landmark which can be identified both on the ground and on the map.

(2) Point the direction-of-travel arrow at the landmark.

(3) Turn the compass housing so that the arrow on the base lines up with the north-facing needle.

(4) Subtract the difference between magnetic north and grid north by moving the compass housing the correct amount.

(5) Place the base plate of the compass on the map with the straight edge touching the landmark from which the bearing was taken.

(6) Without altering the position of the compass housing, turn the base plate on the map until the arrow on the base of the compass housing is exactly parallel to the grid lines.

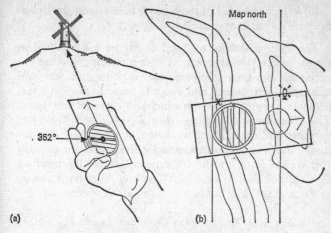

Fig. 13 Finding your exact position on the map

(7) Where the edge of the base plate intersects the line of the footpath is your exact position.

It is obvious that another short cut can be made. Instead of subtracting the magnetic variation, just point the direction-of-travel arrow to the landmark and then turn the compass housing until the north-facing compass needle is pointing at 352° instead of 360°. The process then becomes:

(1) Select a prominent landmark which can be identified on the ground and on the map.

(2) Point the direction-of-travel arrow at the landmark.

(3) Turn the compass housing so that the north-facing needle lines up with 352° (or the appropriate figure).

(4) Place the base plate of the compass on the map with the straight edge touching the landmark from which the bearing was taken.

(5) Without altering the position of the compass housing, pivot the base plate on the landmark until the arrow on the base of the compass housing is exactly parallel to the grid lines.

(6) Where the edge of the base plate intersects the line of the path is your exact position.

The three situations outlined above are fundamental to the use of compass and map. All other conditions of use are variations on these themes; master them and you will quickly become adept and come to regard your map and compass as your best friends which will never let you down. The examples which follow have dispensed with the cumbersome add or subtract for magnetic variation. It is assumed that you will compensate for the part of the country you are in. Note that 8° difference is correct for much of Great Britain but in parts of Wales and Scotland it can be as much as 10°. The information is available on the map.

D. Finding Your Position when Completely Lost: No walker should ever be completely lost unless he has behaved exceptionally foolishly. Being lost usually means that you know to within a mile or two of your position but you need to identify exactly where you are.

Examine the map and note carefully the last time you were absolutely certain of your position. This can usually be done by some physical feature such as a road, stream, church

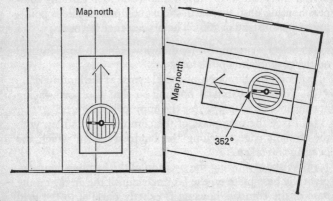

Fig. 14 Orientating the map

or hill, but do make certain that you crossed the road or stream at the right point and that it was the right hill and the right church. Assuming that you can mark on the map your last known position, mark off the direction in which you travelled, if necessary by taking a bearing with your compass. Next, estimate the time taken and/or the distance covered since your last known position and mark this estimated position on the map. You should now have a fairly clear idea of where you are.

Orientate the map by setting the compass at 360° and placing the base plate on the north–south grid lines. Next turn the map and the compass without disturbing the position of the compass until the north facing arrow points to 352° (Figure 14). The map is then set exactly and it should be possible to recognize certain features such as hills (from the shape of their contours) or buildings such as churches.

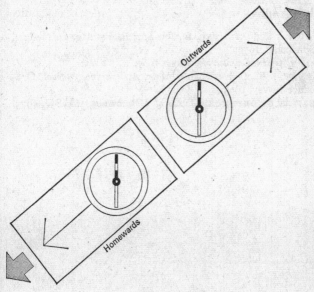

Fig. 15 Back-bearings

Select two features and take a bearing from each of them as described in paragraph C above. Where the two lines intersect is your exact position. You will then be able to take another compass bearing to rejoin the path at some appropriate point. If it proves impossible to locate your position, there is nothing to be done but to retrace your steps until you reach a point which you can definitely identify.

E. Back-Bearings (Figure 15): Sometimes it is necessary to retrace steps or to check the direction of travel by looking backwards towards a feature from which you took your present direction of travel. Merely turn yourself around until the south (white) end of the needle points to the same point on the compass housing (i.e. 360° or 352°) as the north-facing needle did. The direction-of-travel arrow will show you the way you have come.

Bibliography

BROWN, T., and HUNTER, R., *The Spur Book of Map and Compass*, Spurbooks, 1976.

DISLEY, JOHN, *Orienteering*, Faber, 1967.

HARLEY, J. B., *Ordnance Survey Maps, A Descriptive Manual*, Ordnance Survey, 1975.

MINISTRY OF DEFENCE, *Manual of Map Reading*, HMSO, 1973.

In this chapter I shall describe two walks, one in lowland
country and the other in the mountains. The lowland walk
does not actually exist. It is used merely as an exercise in
map-reading and to show clearly the difference between the
detail shown on the 1:50000 map and the 1:25000 map.
Note that only those features which normally appear on the
Ordnance Survey map are shown. Contour and grid lines
have been omitted.

A Walk in Barsetshire

This walk is from Barchester to Winterbourne Stoke. The
1:50000 map was used for planning the walk and the 1:25000
will be used for route-finding. We have never walked these
paths before but, as we know the region is not a popular
walking area and is intensively farmed, we do not expect to
find the paths clearly defined on the ground and so we must
rely on natural features to pinpoint our route.

First let us examine and compare the two maps:

The 1:50000 map (Figure 16) shows the following features:
    roads
    buildings
    streams
    woods

The 1:25000 (Figure 17) shows the following features:
    roads
    buildings

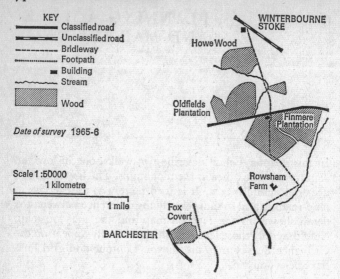

Fig. 16 The 1:50000 map used for route-planning

streams
deciduous woods
coniferous woods
field boundaries

This means that if we want to walk the route using the
1:50000 map we can rely only on walking in the right direction, whereas using the 1:25000 map we shall be able to
progress from field to field, thus ensuring that the line of the
path is followed exactly. Note that we are using the 1:25000
First Series map, which does not show rights of way. We
have checked our map against the Definitive Map (see p.
100) and established from the County Engineer that there
are no diversions or extinguishments. Fortunately, the footpaths and bridleways shown on our map agree with those
shown on the Definitive Map, so no alterations are necessary.
We measure the length of the walk on the 1:50000 map,
using a map measurer or a piece of string and a ruler. The

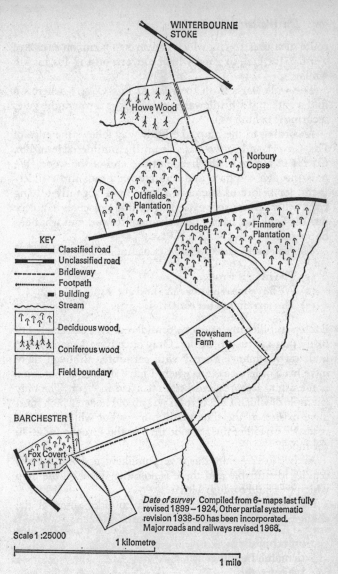

WINTERBOURNE STOKE

Howe Wood

Norbury Copse

Oldfields Plantation

Lodge

Finmere Plantation

KEY

Classified road
Unclassified road
Bridleway
Footpath
Building
Stream
Deciduous wood.
Coniferous wood
Field boundary

Rowsham Farm

BARCHESTER

Fox Covert

Date of survey Compiled from 6- maps last fully revised 1899–1924, Other partial systematic revision 1938-50 has been incorporated. Major roads and railways revised 1968.

Scale 1 :25000

1 kilometre

1 mile

Fig. 17 The 1:25000 map used for route-finding

route measures 10 cm. which converts to 5 km. on a scale of 2 cm. to the km., or 4 ins. which converts on a 1¼-ins. map to 3 miles.

The walk starts from the road at Fox Covert, where we find a gate and a bridleway sign. We pass through the gate, securing it behind us.

According to the map, the bridleway follows the edge of Fox Covert and so we walk down the outside edge of Fox Covert to a gate in the hedge at the end of the wood. We pass through the gate and scratch our heads in bewilderment, for before us stretches a huge field of gently waving corn, whereas we were expecting to find ourselves in a very narrow field. Let us examine the map to work out what has happened.

There are only three possible explanations:

(1) The map is wrong.
(2) We have misread our map and got lost.
(3) The terrain has been altered.

Each possibility must now be considered. It is extremely unlikely that the map is wrong. Only once have I managed to fault the Ordnance Survey with certainty, although there have been other occasions where I have suspected that some non-existent features had been recorded in error. The only example of which I am certain was an old hedge which must have existed at the time of the survey but which was not recorded on either the 1:25000 map or the 1:10560 (6 ins. to the mile).

Are we lost? Again, this is very unlikely, as Fox Covert is readily identifiable and there is no other wood on the map which we could confuse with it.

Has the terrain altered? Let us consider some of the changes man can make on the landscape. He can:

   erect buildings
   demolish buildings
   realign roads
   build new roads

construct reservoirs
fill in canals
abandon railway lines
divert streams
plant new plantations and woods
fell plantations and woods
plant hedges
grub hedges

In this case the most likely explanation is that a hedge or hedges have been grubbed and we have to consider which ones have gone. As far as we can tell from a not very good vantage point the field now looks roughly the shape shown in Figure 18. The long hedge which runs towards the road is

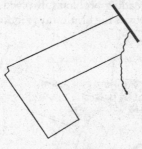

Fig. 18

still there, as is the hedge at which we are standing, although we are suddenly struck by doubts when we realize that the edge of Fox Covert does not project beyond our hedge as shown on the map. Let us consider the possibilities again:

(1) The map is inaccurate (this possibility can be discounted).
(2) The hedge has been moved.
(3) Part of the wood has been felled.

An examination of the hedge shows that it is old, containing many varieties of shrubs and some well-established trees. This proves fairly conclusively that part of Fox Covert has been felled and the 1:50000 map, based on a much later survey, shows the footpath crossing the bridleway running outside Fox Covert whereas the 1:25000 map shows the footpath emerging from the wood.

We have now identified two hedges and from the size of the field we can deduce that the hedge which formed the boundary of the narrow enclosure has been grubbed. But even if we imagine our map without that hedge the shape of the field is still wrong, so we have to consider whether any other hedges have been removed. We can see that the field is L-shaped and this gives us the clue, for we can now see that another hedge running at right angles to the bridleway has been removed.

Although we do not plan to follow it, let us turn our attention to the map-reading problems involved in following the footpath which crosses the bridleway (Figure 19).

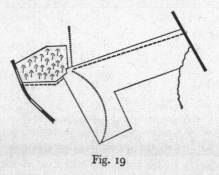

Fig. 19

Using the 1:25000 anyone travelling in a southerly direction would expect to pass the edge of Fox Covert and then to walk up the right-hand headland of a now non-existent hedge (a headland is a path that follows a field boundary). When the hedge was grubbed the farmer should have applied to divert the path along the other headland because the path makes for the corner of the field, and his own, as well as recreational, interests would be better served by a sensible diversion. Without accurate surveying instruments it would be impossible to follow the true line of the path, so in these circumstances it would be better to follow the headland route.

To return to our bridleway. We can now walk down the left-hand headland to a gate at the bottom of the field. After passing through the gate we see that according to the map the path moves slightly away from the headland. However, there is a tractor trail running to the road and following the left-hand headland so, as the field is full of wheat and the true line of the path not restored, we follow the tractor trail to the road.

At the road we turn right and look for a bridleway sign on the left-hand side. There is no signpost but we can see a gate which must be the one we want because it is roughly halfway between the point from where we emerged onto the road and the little bridge which carries the road over the stream. We pass through the gate and head diagonally across the field to a gate we can see in the hedge opposite. The path now heads across the field to the junction of the hedge and stream, where we find a wide gap leading into the next field. The fields on each side of the gap are pasture and there is no sign on the ground of the route of the bridleway. Anyone using the 1:50000 map would be quite unable to determine which side of the hedge to follow.

However, we are using the 1:25000 map and so we confidently follow the left-hand headland to a gate which leads into the next field, where the bridleway follows the right-hand headland. At the top of this field we reach Finmere Plantation. Here again we notice some changes. The map shows this as a deciduous wood, but changes have taken place, as shown in Figure 20.

We find there is no proper access through the fence which forms the boundary of the plantation. We manage to scramble over, but a horse would not get through. At this point we pause to establish that we are on the line of the path and, having satisfied ourselves that we are, we make a note of the grid reference and the circumstances so that we can report the matter to the County Engineer of Barsetshire.

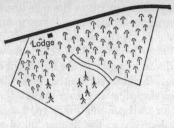

Fig. 20

We follow the left-hand headland of the clearing in the plantation and note that some young conifers have been planted, probably by the Forestry Commission. At the end of the clearing we come to another fence with no access, so we make another note to inform the County Engineer and then reach a broad forest track on the other side of the fence. As this track appears to be about the right distance from the edge of the wood we think it must be the path, so we turn right and follow it. A number of forest tracks not marked on the map cross the path, but as the path we are following seems to be going in the right direction we do not trouble to confirm it by a compass bearing. After a few hundred yards our confidence is confirmed when we reach a clearing around the Lodge. We keep the Lodge on our left and find a gate and bridleway sign on the main road.

On the other side of the road we see a gate and bridleway sign, so we follow the path down the headland to a gated culvert which crosses the stream and then follow it. According to the map the path crosses the stream again at a foot-bridge and sure enough we come to a wide farm bridge solidly constructed of sleepers laid on stout timbers and obviously designed to accommodate tractors. We cross the bridge and find a farm track curving away to the far right-hand corner of the field (see Figure 21).

Before automatically following the farm track our natural caution asserts itself. On checking the map we find that the path runs along the edge of Howe Wood and we can now see a gate on the edge of the wood. We ignore the farm track and

Fig. 21

make for the gate, entering a narrow lane bordered by hedges which leads into a field. The path continues in the same direction to the corner of the field to a gate in the hedge bordering the road. Beside the gate is a house, which causes us some confusion as it is not marked on the map, and for a moment or two we wonder if we have gone wrong. However, we can now see that it is a modern house, probably built after the survey for the 1:25000 map, and reference to the 1:50000 map confirms that a house should be there. We are now on the outskirts of Winterbourne Stoke and walk down the road into the village.

This imaginary walk illustrates many of the problems of map-reading likely to be encountered in lowland country. There is no doubt that the thousands of miles of hedges that have been grubbed in recent years to enlarge the fields to make them more convenient to farm causes route-finding problems for walkers. Those described on the walk above are a comparatively simple exercise in deduction. The following real-life example is much more complicated. Figure 22 shows some fields and the path crossing them as they were at the time they were surveyed. Figure 23 shows the modern field pattern with eight hedges removed. It is very difficult to cope with situations like this. Sometimes by standing on the top of a stile or a gate it is possible to work out what has happened, but in the absence of any feature such as a building or road which can be used as a point of reference, the only thing to do is to take a compass bearing and march across the field.

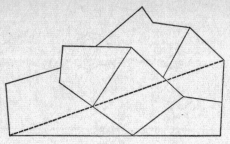

Fig. 22

Fortunately, this path goes in a straight line. Had it changed direction at each of the old hedges the problem would have been very much more difficult (see Figure 24). It would have been necessary to take a compass bearing to where the hedge used to be, then, using the ruler on the edge of the Silva compass, to measure the distance to the non-existent hedge. One millimetre on the 1:25000 map represents 50 metres on the ground, so if you know the number of paces you take to cover 50 metres you will be able to count the appropriate number of paces and be able to arrive at the point where the hedge used to be with reasonable accuracy. If this process of taking a compass bearing, measuring the distance on the map and then counting the appropriate number of paces to cover the required distance is repeated at every field boundary you will sooner or later

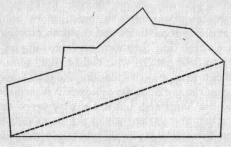

Fig. 23

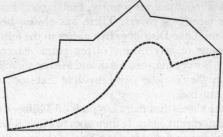

Fig. 24

arrive at a feature that you will recognize from the map. If you follow this procedure carefully you will be surprised at how well you can stay on course.

This method of route-finding is so useful it is worth taking a surveyor's tape into the countryside and measuring 50 metres. Walk up and down the distance several times using your normal walking stride and counting the number of paces. Take the average of six attempts and note the result so that it can be slipped into your compass case. As your stride will be a different length on flat pasture, ploughing, ascending steep hills and descending steep hills it is worth taking measurements for each type of terrain.

In downland country in some parts of England field boundaries are few and far between. Paths in this kind of country are often well marked but a compass may be necessary, using such features as buildings, woods and copses to follow the line of the path. The shapes of the hills lend themselves to establishing the proper route. In hilly country route-finding is more nearly akin to route-finding in mountainous country although, of course, the terrain is less rugged and streams are very rare.

A Walk in the Lake District

This is a circular walk from the New Dungeon Ghyll Hotel (grid reference NY 296064) and one that recalls particularly happy memories.

As this is mountainous country, the 1:50000 map is quite adequate (see back cover). There has always been a tradition in the Lake District of free access to the fells irrespective of rights of way. Many of the paths marked on the Ordnance Survey map are black and are not therefore rights of way, but they may be used providing that stock and game are not disturbed.

The map shows that there is a path up Millbeck to Stickle Tarn and Sergeant Man. It then goes to High Rise, Thunacar Knott, Pavey Ark, Harrison Stickle, Pike o' Stickle and down to the New Dungeon Ghyll Hotel again. There is a spot height of 97 metres (282 ft) marked on the map near the hotel and the loftiest point of the walk, High Rise (762 metres; 2,500 ft), is 2½ miles away as the crow flies, so there must be some stiff climbing, which the closeness of the contour lines confirms. According to the map measurer, the distance is 7 miles, but it is likely to be more than this because, in mountainous country with steep slopes, every turn of the path cannot be indicated.

Applying Naismith's formula we calculate time taken to be: 7 miles at 3 mph = 2 hours 20 minutes, plus 2,500 ft of climbing at 1 hour per 2,000 ft = 1 hour 15 minutes. The total time is therefore 3 hours 35 minutes, and we allow ourselves an additional 1½ hours for lunch and time to admire the view, making a total of 5 hours.

Note that once Sergeant Man is reached, there is not much variation in height until leaving Pike o' Stickle, from which there is a very steep descent to the New Dungeon Ghyll Hotel.

The day has dawned clear with a few clouds. We telephone the local weather station (Windermere 5151) which gives weather and walking conditions on the fells for the Lake District. The forecast is mainly fair with occasional heavy showers and the lowest cloud cover at 2,000 ft. It is likely to be wet underfoot and the becks high because of the recent heavy rain – altogether an ideal day for a walk in the mountains! Naturally, we wear boots and breeches and pack into the rucksack cagoules, overtrousers, spare sweaters, plenty of food, including an emergency ration of Kendal Mint Cake, lemon squash, maps, survival bags and first-aid kit. Attached to lanyards we have a compass and a whistle. At the hotel we leave a written record of names, addresses, route to be taken and the estimated time of arrival back at the hotel, so that if we fail to return the mountain rescue team will have a clear idea of where to search.

The path follows the beck behind the hotel. There are a number of notices stating that, owing to heavy use, the path has been eroded and alternative paths made. The path up to Stickle Tarn, over boulders and rocks, is very clear. Its steepness causes us to pause frequently to regain our breath. Stickle Tarn is a beautiful spot, with Pavey Ark behind it standing like a sheer cliff. The map shows that the path follows the eastern edge of the tarn and crosses the beck which is fed by the tarn. After the recent rain, the beck is in spate and fairly foams over its bed of boulders, making the crossing of it rather precarious as there is no bridge.

From the edge of the tarn, the cairned path can be seen zigzagging away in the general direction of Sergeant Man, which can now be identified from the map. The map shows that three paths leave Stickle Tarn at approximately the same point. One goes almost due east towards Blea Crag, one goes due north to the eastern end of Pavey Ark and ours heads in a generally north-easterly direction. We soon identify our path and follow the cairns, climbing steadily but not too steeply. Sergeant Man is reached in about 2 hours after leaving the car park and in time for lunch. From the map we can identify Codale Tarn, Easedale Tarn, Coniston Water, Esthwaite Water and Windermere as well as Helvellyn and Coniston Old Man. All around are clouds and some of the higher summits are covered in cloud and mist.

We are now feeling chilly, so we press on for a short distance to a cairn which we assume at first to be the summit of High Rise. But on checking the map we find that there should be a trig point at the top and then we see it about 300 yds away. High Rise has no prominent summit and is rather a disappointment after Sergeant Man. There is a row of iron stakes which is intriguing us and the map suggests that they must indicate the boundary of the land owned by the National Trust.

We plan now to walk along Thunacar Knott to Pavey Ark. The ground is fairly level but drops away steeply on the western side. We see clouds approaching which are obviously low enough to envelop us. There are no cairns marking the path so, to be on the safe side, we take a compass bearing from the map along the line of the path, which is straight for nearly a mile. As it will be easy walking, we know that in 20 minutes we shall be ready to take another bearing to bring us onto Pavey Ark should the clouds not lift. It is now raining and the mist is drifting in so we put on our cagoules and start walking, following the compass bearing. After ten minutes or so, the clouds roll back and we find ourselves on the true line of the path. We can now see the route to the top of Pavey Ark bending away to the west and we follow it. This is a very easy stretch until we reach the last few hundred yards, where there is a jumble of rocks and we have to scramble up to the summit.

We find ourselves standing on a natural rampart – and what a view! Pavey Ark is 2,288 ft high, and 1,200 ft below its almost vertical wall is Stickle Tarn. The view covers an area of hundreds of square miles, stretching as far as Morecambe Bay. The next summit is Harrison Stickle, clearly visible from Pavey Ark about half a mile away. The path is cairned but care is needed over the boulders which cover the surface. The last hundred feet or so to the summit is quite a tough scramble and there is no one well-defined route. Our next objective is Pike o' Stickle, another half mile away and clearly visible with a broad track crossing the turf and peat. There are splendid views to the west and we recognize Scafell Pike, the highest mountain in England, Bowfell and the massive head of Great Gable. Suddenly, the clouds close in. There is a brief hailstorm, and even though it is the end of July the hailstones lie for some time before melting. Descending Pike o' Stickle, we find a family, including two little boys aged about five, sheltering from the hail under an overhanging rock. All have boots and cagoules and are obviously enjoying their walk.

The descent to the New Dungeon Ghyll Hotel now commences. Examine the map closely. It will be seen that the path at first follows Dungeon Ghyll but then moves away westward from the beck. The cairned path is well defined but it is very steep and tricky, with some loose scree. After some time we learn that climbing is much easier than descending and we let our knees go slack to cushion the effect of the steep slope.

At this point we notice a family group comprising a grandmother, mother and father and a child of about ten. They appear to be motorists who have decided to explore a footpath and got themselves into difficulties. Grandmother in particular is wearing very unsuitable white boots and has to descend the steep slope by sliding on her bottom with her arms held by her children. Fortunately they are not far from the road, but had they strayed further, or if it was the end of the day, they could have been in serious trouble.

Near the hotel, the path crosses Dungeon Ghyll and as there is no bridge it is necessary to leap from boulder to boulder to cross the beck. We now reach the hotel and our walk is over. All that remains to be done is to notify our hotel that we have returned safely, take a bath, change and enjoy our dinner.

Every square inch of this beautiful country of ours is owned by someone. There is no such thing as waste ground; there is only land that is not well kept and thus becomes derelict. Whenever you are out walking you are crossing land that belongs to someone. He will have a great interest in it, as it probably provides his livelihood. Because this is so, there is sometimes a conflict of interests between the farmer or land-owner, who is naturally interested in the efficient use of the land, and those who seek their recreation in the countryside. These interests are not always easy to harmonize. Matters would be less difficult if more walkers had some understanding of modern farming methods and the ways of the countryside and if farmers paid more attention to their legal obligations towards footpaths and bridleways.

Beauty is said to be in the eye of the beholder, and the sight of a field of golden corn or a herd of fat bullocks is more pleasing to a farmer than a barren fellside or inhospitable mountain. It is a farmer's natural instinct to improve the land until it will bear crops and he has little sympathy with those conservationists who want to leave certain areas in their wild state.

Barbed Wire and Electric Fences

Barbed wire is a perennial problem for walkers, yet it is the farmer's friend. He uses wire because farm animals like to push against obstacles in the hope of breaking through; barbed wire and electric fences prevent them from pushing.

Farmers with attested herds of cattle have to prevent the possibility of infection from a neighbouring herd by double fencing, and barbed wire provides the ideal answer. Nevertheless, barbed wire without proper access through it constitutes an obstruction and is illegal on the line of a path. The problem can be overcome by the provision of a stile or gate through the fence or by a 'hoosier'. In this device, the fence has a movable post with a loop of wire on it which drops over a fixed post, thus allowing the walker to undo the wire and fasten it again behind him. Electric fences and single-strand barbed-wire fences can be sleeved with rubber hose.

Damage

Farming is very capital intensive and there is often a lot of expensive machinery lying around unattended. This makes some farmers feel very vulnerable and they fear that large groups of people crossing their land may damage machinery, crops and stock. In my experience, most farmers are friendly towards individual walkers but suspicious of large groups. It is one of the curiosities of human nature that people in groups tend not to behave as well as each one of them would individually. Large numbers of people walking together can cause considerable damage unless they walk considerately. Forty people climbing over a field gate rather than bothering to open it will not improve it, especially if it is climbed at the latched end so that the full weight is taken on the hinges. A ten-stone person climbing a gate 10 ft long with hinges 2 ft 6 ins. apart will exert a leverage of half a ton on the hinges. No gate can stand this kind of misuse for long and field gates now cost in the region of £40. The same group walking carelessly four or five abreast will damage wet pasture, for too many walkers fail to recognize that grass is a valuable crop.

Dogs

The legislation covering paths does not include any mention of dogs, but in the case of *Regina* versus *Matthias* in 1861 it was held to be legal to push a pram on a public path, providing the path was physically capable of accommodating the pram, on the grounds that a pram was a 'natural accompaniment' of a pedestrian. Presumably, the argument could be extended to include dogs. But dogs can be a menace to stock, for it is a natural instinct in most dogs to chase anything that is nervous of them. Apart from the obvious danger that this will encourage the dog to worry sheep and perhaps eventually kill, there is a serious risk of dairy cows going dry and of pregnant animals aborting. Even the best-behaved dog must be kept on a leash when there is stock about. Under the Farm Animals Act, 1971, farmers have a right to shoot dogs found worrying animals if that is the only way to prevent it happening. I know of one case where a farmer found a pedigree dog chasing his sheep and warned the owner that the dog would be shot if found worrying stock again. The owner indicated that only a barbarian would shoot such a valuable animal and he would have no hesitation in suing if the farmer were to be so foolish. A few days later, a Landrover drew up at the owner's home and the bodies of a sheep, horribly mutilated, and the shot dog were deposited on the front doorstep. No legal action was taken because the farmer was acting within his rights.

Fires

In many people's minds there is a romantic view of backwoodsmen sitting round a camp fire cooking their evening meal. This indeed is common practice in the wilderness areas of the United States and is perfectly proper there, but make a golden rule *never* to light fires in this country. It is a practice fraught with danger practically anywhere except perhaps on the beach. Lighting fires in cultivated country is unforgivable and is done only by the ignorant and stupid. A farmer finding anyone lighting fires on his land is likely to hand out a tongue lashing which will not easily be forgotten. Irresponsible behaviour will quickly alienate sympathetic farmers. As we have seen, if hot food is needed there are many lightweight portable stoves on the market – some of them costing under a pound – which can be used in complete safety. All modern stoves burn clean fuel so they have the added advantage over camp fires in that they do not soil the outside of the cooking utensils.

Litter

The litter sometimes to be found in popular walking areas is a disgrace to the walking fraternity. Along the whole length of the Pennine Way there are piles of tin cans around certain cairns, as well as innumerable paper wrappings. I once spent nearly a week following someone who kept dropping an unusual brand of confectionery wrapping, making a trail that was quite distinctive. No doubt he was unaware of how offensive I found his behaviour. A civilized person never deposits litter.

Pubs

Part of the pleasure of walking is the occasional visit to a country pub. Walkers are likely to arrive travel-stained, with muddy boots and perhaps soaking wet, for a friendly pub is a pleasant haven in the rain. Some landlords welcome walkers but others prefer not to have them as they are trying to attract a different clientele. It is their privilege to do this as they are not obliged to serve anyone if they do not wish to. I get some wry amusement as I pass a pub that I sometimes use at lunch time during the week, properly dressed with well-polished shoes, knowing full well that I would not be welcome on Sundays in my boots and breeches. It is advisable to use the public bar and, unless the pub caters especially for walkers, to leave boots outside the door. Most landlords insist that large rucksacks must be left outside.

Groups of walkers are likely to be high spirited and noisy, which may not matter in a bar frequented by walkers but would not be popular in a quiet country pub where the locals are likely to resent any hint of rowdyism.

Farm Animals

It is surprising how many people are nervous of cattle. Apart from bulls, and cows with newly born calves, cattle are normally absolutely harmless but very inquisitive. Heifers and bullocks in particular are skittish and will come galloping across the field to investigate strangers, but they will come skidding to a halt a few yards away and will then follow at a safe distance. Dogs can be an embarrassment because cattle will often form a defensive ring and attempt to menace the dog. Very occasionally horses may kick or bite, pigs are reputed to be able to inflict a savage bite, rams and billy goats can be belligerent and geese noisy and aggressive, but I have never heard of a walker being attacked by these animals.

Bulls are the most dangerous animals to be found on farms and most counties have a by-law prohibiting the free running of bulls in fields crossed by public paths, but sometimes the by-law is ignored. No bull is to be trusted, but the most dangerous are the dairy breeds, particularly Friesians, Jerseys and Guernseys. Bulls usually signify their annoyance by a roaring or bellowing noise which is quite different from the lowing of cows. The safest thing to do if a bull is encountered is to get out of the field fast without attracting the attention of the animal. All cattle are interested in humans and it does not follow that a bull is threatening merely because it comes towards you, but the wise take no chances! Fortunately, the bull is a clumsy animal and, providing you keep calm, it should be possible to dodge if it does charge. Walkers should take comfort from the fact that in the past twenty years no one, other than farm workers, has been killed by a bull.

Occasionally, the walker will discover farm animals in

trouble. Unless it is easy to do something for them, like releasing them from a wire fence, it is better to inform the nearest farm. Make a note of the exact position of the animal and of any identification marks so that a clear description can be given to the farmer. If it is not his animal he will know to whom it belongs and will telephone him. Sometimes lambs appear to be lost and will be found bleating piteously, but do not touch them because the mother is almost certain to be near by and if her lamb is moved she may never find it.

Sheep sometimes get onto their broad flat backs and are unable to regain their feet. To right the animal, kneel beside it and seize one front leg and pull it across its chest. This will bring the animal onto its side and it will be able to get to its feet.

Diseases of Animals

All farm animals are subject to disease. The most virulent and feared are brucellosis, foot and mouth disease, fowl pest, and swine vesicular disease. Under the Diseases of Animals Act, 1950, temporary orders extinguishing rights of way may be made, but in any case considerate walkers will avoid areas known to be affected and respect notices forbidding entry because of disease. Unless there is an outbreak of disease there is no likelihood of walkers spreading infection except by inexcusable behaviour such as leaving gates open. Rational arguments that no order has been made forbidding the use of paths during an outbreak of disease are unlikely to convince a farmer desperately worried about losing his stock and livelihood. Farmers grow attached to their animals and have enormous justifiable pride in the splendid pedigree animals that they rear; never put them at risk.

Brucellosis or contagious abortion is a disease which affects cattle, causing cows to abort, and it may be responsible for undulant fever in humans if the untreated milk of infected cows is drunk. The disease can be carried by dogs, by wild animals and by boots which have come into contact with an infected foetus or afterbirth. A government scheme exists for the eradication of brucellosis which registers herds which are free from the disease and which are constantly tested to ensure their continual freedom. Attested herds have to be separated from other cattle by double fencing and this is one of the main reasons for refraining from cutting barbed wire obstructing paths. It is much better to take the matter up with the farmer, County Council or Parish Council as detailed in Chapter 9.

Foot and mouth disease is a highly infectious disease of cattle, sheep and pigs. Infected animals become feverish, develop blisters in the mouth and on the feet, readily salivate and become lame. It is a notifiable disease and is controlled by the wholesale slaughter of cattle, sheep and pigs on the premises, whether or not they are infected, and the movement of animals for a very wide area around the infected herd is prohibited. The speed with which the disease can spread is frightening and during the bad outbreak of 1967–68 thousands of beasts were destroyed and their carcasses burned in huge funeral pyres. The virus is very tenacious and can be spread by wind, rain and snow. Walkers should be aware that it can be spread by clothing, especially by the boots, and paths in infected areas should never be used during the outbreak.

Fowl pest is a disease of poultry spread by a highly infectious virus. Since vaccination against the disease is now widespread, it is much less common than once it was. Fowl pest can be spread by clothing and walkers should avoid infected farms and broiler houses.

Swine vesicular disease is very similar to foot and mouth disease but is peculiar to pigs and first occurred in this country in 1972. The only way to control an outbreak is to slaughter all pigs on the premises and to control the movement of pigs.

It is considered possible to transmit the disease on clothing, so walkers should avoid infected areas.

Trespass

In many parts of the country, it is quite normal for some villagers to roam at will through the fields. They have no right to do this except with the permission of the landowner, but they are tolerated because they are country folk who would never walk where they would cause damage. Walkers sometimes meet them in the fields and may be puzzled when informed that they go where they like, for it must be a fundamental rule, strictly adhered to by all walkers, *never* to stray from the right of way without the express permission of the farmer or landowner. Few farmers are likely to object to picnicking in pasture near the line of the path but the considerate person will leave no trace of his meal behind him. Animals may die if they swallow plastic bags and be severely injured by tin cans and broken bottles. Keep a plastic bag in your rucksack so that you can carry your litter home and dispose of it properly, for the countryside is not a rubbish dump.

Anyone who strays from the line of the path is trespassing unless it is necessary to circumvent an obstruction caused by the landowner, but this does not entitle a walker to trespass on the property of a different landowner. Trespassing is not an offence punishable at law but is a civil wrong or 'tort', and anyone causing damage in the course of trespassing can be sued for damages. Landowners have a right to insist that trespassers leave their land, or return to the right of way, and may use any reasonable and necessary force to compel them. An injunction can be issued against anyone who persists in trespassing.

It is comparatively rare for walkers using rights of way to be approached by landowners and told that they are trespassing. Providing you are absolutely sure of your facts, and especially if you have a copy of the Definitive Map with you (see p. 100) and have checked with the local authority that there has been no extinguishment or diversion, you should discuss the matter courteously and, if agreement cannot be reached, politely but firmly insist on using the public path. But if the situation gets out of hand, it is probably better to ask for the name and address of the landowner and of the person who actually stops you and report the matter in detail to the local authority.

Only once have I been prevented from using a right of way. I was surveying a public bridleway for a footpath guide which I was writing when I was stopped by a farmer at the entrance to his stockyard. He denied that there was a right of way even though I showed him the Definitive Map and, as he had obstructed the path by building a dutch barn over it, I asked for his name so that I could take the matter up with the County Council. Three days later he received a letter from me sent by recorded delivery outlining the legal position of public rights of way and a photocopy of the relevant section of the Definitive Map. I advised him to contact the local secretary of the National Farmers' Union and the County Engineer's department for confirmation that a right of way ran through his farm. Copies of the letter and enclosures were sent to the NFU and the County Council and within a few days the NFU had arranged a meeting between their Secretary, the farmer and myself at which it was acknowledged that the right of way existed but was obstructed and impassable and that a suitable diversion would be sought.

Wild Flowers and Fruits

Wild flowers must never be picked, but it is permissible to take wild fruits under certain conditions. Mushrooms etc. which grow on the line of the path may be taken, but you can be sued for damages by the landowner if you take anything from his land that is not on the line of the path. However, it is apparently not stealing to take wild mushrooms and fruits even if they are not on the path unless you sell them for gain or reward. In practice, of course, it is customary for blackberries to be picked from hedgerows, sometimes in large quantities, and very few landowners would object, but some farmers get very cross if the mushrooms they were expecting for their own breakfast are taken. Never, under any circumstances, pick anything cultivated, not even a single ear of corn.

The Country Code

The guide to good behaviour is the Country Code which, unfortunately, is curiously worded and needs some explanation.

(1) Guard against all risks of fire. Never light fires and always break your dead matches in half to make certain that they are out.

(2) Fasten all gates. Unless you find an open gate secured. Never swing on gates and if they will not open climb them only at the hinge end.

(3) Keep dogs under proper control. Exceptionally obedient dogs may not need to be on a leash when there is no stock about but *all* dogs *must* be on a leash in the presence of farm animals and game.

(4) Keep to paths across farmland. Always keep to the path unless walking in an area where access agreements have been negotiated.

(5) Avoid damaging fences, hedges and walls. Dry stone walls are very vulnerable. Never climb them or remove any stones from them. Building and repairing dry stone walls is a highly skilled craft.

(6) Leave no litter – take it home. Cans and bottles can injure the feet of animals and plastic bags can be fatal if swallowed. The Americans sum it up in a neat phrase 'pack your trash'. You brought the rubbish, so take it home again!

(7) Protect wild life, wild plants and trees. Never pick flowers or dig them up. Never damage trees or carve into the bark and never interfere with nests or take eggs.

(8) Go carefully on country roads. Drive carefully and if on foot always keep in single file facing oncoming traffic.

(9) Respect the life of the countryside. Behave decorously and greet politely everyone you meet.

(10) Safeguard water supplies. Never pollute or foul reservoirs, lakes or rivers.

THE FOOTPATH AND BRIDLEWAY NETWORK IN ENGLAND AND WALES

There are approximately one hundred thousand miles of public paths in England and Wales, forming a network that covers the two countries. It is possible, and John Hillaby in his book *Journey through Britain* has proved it, to walk the length and breadth of our beautiful land on public paths.

Paths were established in prehistoric times long before the Romans built our first proper road system. They were used for trading purposes and linked centres where the essentials of prehistoric life were to be found – salt, flint, pottery etc. Normally, they followed high-level routes – travelling was easier on hills because the low-lying land had not yet been drained. The long-distance Ridgeway Path follows a prehistoric trading route for part of its length, from Avebury in Wiltshire to Ivinghoe in Buckinghamshire. During the Middle Ages, the land was drained and reclaimed from the forest which, to a large extent, covered the country and then paths were used as a means of getting about the countryside by the shortest route. Most walkers will have observed that paths usually provide the more direct route from village to village and often are considerably shorter than the road route.

From the nineteenth century onwards, paths were also used for recreation. The novels of Jane Austen and Thomas Hardy abound in references to walks being taken for recreational purposes on public paths. During those dreadful years between the two world wars, thousands of the unemployed left the industrial cities of the north each weekend to forget their unhappy lot for a while by walking the hills of

Yorkshire, Derbyshire and Northumbria. Many of the battles to gain access to the moors were won at this time by men being prepared to go to prison rather than be excluded from some of the fells.

Definitive Maps

In the immediate post-war years, the government decided to tidy the jungle of case law which largely governed the use of paths. The National Parks and Access to the Countryside Act, 1949 laid upon the County Councils a statutory duty to compile and publish Definitive Maps showing all public paths on a scale not less than 1:25000 (2½ ins. to the mile). The County Council normally invited each parish council to survey the paths in its parish and from this information the draft map was compiled. Later this was published as the Provisional Rights of Way Map and objections were invited.

At this stage, it was possible to assert that a path shown on the Provisional Map was not a right of way and had only been used by the public with the permission of the landowner. In some cases, the exact line of the right of way was disputed. Did it go one side or the other of a hedge? It was possible, also, to get paths not shown on the Provisional Map included as rights of way, for the person who had supplied the information about paths in the parish perhaps had been unaware that this particular path had been used by the public as a right of way.

The evidence was then sifted and negotiations took place between the interested parties on any points in dispute. If it was not possible to resolve any dispute by negotiation, a public inquiry was held by an Inspector appointed by the Minister of Town and Country Planning. The Inspector submitted the results of his inquiry to the Minister, who made a decision in the light of the evidence. The Definitive Map was then published incorporating all the decisions made resulting from the publication of the Provisional Map. All counties now have Definitive Maps except Bedfordshire (part of county definitive) and Gloucestershire (most of county definitive).

The importance of the Definitive Map cannot be exaggerated. It provides conclusive evidence in law of the existence of a right of way at the time the map was made. A path that appears on the Definitive Map is always a right of way, even if it was included by mistake, unless an extinguishment or diversion is granted, which can only be done by due legal process. Even though a path may be overgrown with vegetation, obstructed by barbed wire, have houses built across it and be ploughed up, there is still a right to use it, and the local authority, which has a statutory duty ' to assert and protect the rights of the public to the use and enjoyment of all highways and to prevent, as far as possible, the stopping-up or obstruction of those highways ', can use its powers to have the path opened for public use.

The Definitive Map can be seen at the County Council offices, usually in the Surveyor's Department. The local public library may well have a copy and in any case will be able to tell you where a copy may be seen.

Some counties use the 1:25000 map, others prefer the 1:10580 map. Whichever map is used, footpaths and bridleways are drawn in and allocated a number which is usually done parish by parish. Thus, each path can be readily identified – for example, Aylesbury 7. Counties which use the 1:25000 map may publish copies for sale to the public. Unfortunately, with a map of this scale it is not always entirely clear exactly where the path runs unless the rights of way have been drawn meticulously. If the Definitive Map is based on the 1:10580 map, there should never be any doubt of the true line of the path, but it is more difficult to publish that map for sale to the public.

When local government was re-organized in 1974, County Councils were allowed to enter into agreements with District Councils to delegate some or all of their functions. It is possible to establish the practice in any given authority by inquiring from the County Surveyor or at the public library.

Details of diversion and extinguishment orders made since the Definitive Map was made can usually be obtained from the County Council.

Rights of way are shown on the following Ordnance Survey maps: 1:25000 (Second Series only), 1:50000 and 1:63360. In cultivated country where diversions and extinguishments are much more common, it is essential to use the 1:25000 map for walking. It is a sensible plan to mark public paths on your own map from the details obtained from an examination of the Definitive Map.

Rationalization of Public Paths

The National Farmers' Union is committed to a rationalization of the footpath and bridleway network which would result in far fewer paths especially in lowland cultivated areas. It is argued that the existing pattern of paths is not necessary, as few people use them and they are inimicable to efficient agriculture. The problem needs to be considered carefully, and the natural instinct of most walkers to reject out of hand the concept of rationalization is probably unwise. Walkers with an intimate knowledge of paths in an intensively farmed area know that where fields are crossed by two or more paths, as sometimes happens (I know of one twelve-acre field with no less than five paths across it!), a slight re-arrangement can often be made without detriment to recreational interests. The claim that paths should be extinguished if nobody uses them cannot be taken seriously if the paths concerned are not restored after ploughing, are obstructed by barbed wire and growing crops, and have bulls loose on them. Experience shows that paths are well used in those parts of the country where farmers observe the law meticulously and fulfil their legal obligations towards public paths.

There are varying and often exaggerated opinions as to how much farming land is 'lost' to public paths. At the 1974 Annual General Meeting of the Commons, Open Spaces and Footpaths Preservation Society, the then Vice President of the NFU stated that if all the land occupied by footpaths in England and Wales were given over to food production, it would be possible to feed another half million people. He went on to say that public paths occupy 500,000 acres of good land and that food is more important than paths. This statement was later admitted to be inaccurate. It is generally agreed that there are about 100,000 miles of public paths in England and Wales, so according to NFU arithmetic, assuming that all land occupied by paths were capable of being cultivated, every path, on average, would have to be 40 ft wide! The true figure is difficult to calculate accurately because many paths cross non-productive land such as woods, forest, moorland, fell and common, and some paths are used as tractor trails by the farmer himself. An estimate of 30,000 acres of productive land 'lost' to public paths is probably much nearer the truth, which is the area covered by one hundred medium-sized farms – a small price to pay for such an invaluable amenity which can be used by the whole population.

Diversion and Extinguishment of Paths

It is obvious that from time to time it is necessary for paths to be diverted or extinguished to allow building development to take place or for the land to be used more efficiently, and provision has been made for such eventualities. In order to maintain the path network it is essential that any attempt to divert a path unofficially should be vigorously opposed, otherwise the diversion will not appear on maps and a great deal of ill-will and confusion will be caused.

Paths must only be extinguished and diverted by due legal process and the main provisions are set out below.

Highways Act, 1959, Section 110 This enables a local authority (including a National Park Board) to close a public path if the path is not necessary for public use.

Section 111 This enables a local authority (including a National Park Board) to divert a public path to make it more commodious to the public or to secure the efficient use of land.

Procedure

The legal procedure for extinguishing or diverting a public path under Sections 110 and 111 involves:

(1) if the County Council makes the order it must consult the District Council

(2) if the District Council makes the order it must consult the County Council

(3) if the path is within a National Park the body making the order must consult the Countryside Commission

(4) the draft order must be advertised in the *London Gazette*, at least one local newspaper and at the ends of the sections of path affected

(5) the advertisement must state the general effect of the order and must indicate where a map showing the path in question can be inspected and allow at least twenty-eight days for objections to be filed

(6) a copy of the order must be sent to any Parish or Community Council within whose area any part of the path affected lies

(7) if no objections are received within the twenty-eight days allowed or if any objections made are subsequently withdrawn, the authority making the order can confirm the order

(8) if objections are made, the matter is referred to the Secretary of State who may hold a public inquiry or, with the approval of the objectors, may deal with the matter in other ways

(9) the inspector appointed by the Secretary of State makes his report and the Minister will then announce his decision.

Section 108   Under this Section of the Act, a Highway Authority may make an application to the magistrates' courts for an order: (a) to extinguish a highway on the grounds that it is unnecessary, or (b) to divert a highway so as to make it more commodious to the public. A Highway Authority must inform: (a) the District Council, (b) the Parish Council, Community Council or the Chairman of the Parish Meeting, of its intention to apply for an order. If any of the above bodies objects to the application, then the Highway Authority cannot proceed. An advertisement giving details of the proposed extinguishment must appear in the *London Gazette*, at least one local newspaper and at the ends of the path. Any objectors must appear personally before the magistrates to state their case.

This Section of the Act is used primarily for extinguishing or diverting a carriageway, green lane, a road used as a public path (RUPP) or a highway open to all traffic, as Sections 110 and 111 apply only to footpaths and bridleways. It may also be used for extinguishing vehicular rights and thus downgrading the highway to a bridleway or footpath.

Sections 9 and 13   The Secretary of State has powers to make orders extinguishing or diverting public paths which are affected by the construction of motorways and trunk roads. What often happens in such situations is that several paths are diverted so that they cross the new road at one point by means of a tunnel or bridge. The procedure to be adopted is as follows:

(1) The draft order must be published in the *London Gazette* and in at least one local newspaper as well as on the path.

(2) The advertisement must state where a map showing the path can be seen and must allow a period of six weeks for objections to be filed.

(3) If the Secretary of State considers an objection is not relevant (e.g. the real reason for objecting is to prevent the construction of the road) he may disregard the objection.

(4) The Secretary of State may hold a public inquiry if valid objections are made.

(5) If an alternative route for a diverted path is suggested,

then the Secretary of State can require the objector to state his proposed route at least fourteen days before the public inquiry is held.

(6) After the inquiry is held, the Secretary of State must publish his decision in the *London Gazette* and in at least one local newspaper.

Town and Country Planning Act, 1971, Section 209 Under this Section, the Secretary of State can make an order to extinguish or divert any highway to allow development to take place.

Section 210 Under this Section, country planning authorities and district planning authorities are given the power to extinguish or divert a path to permit development to take place in accordance with planning permission. The planning authority has the power to create an alternative path as distinct from a diverted path.

Section 211 This Section gives the Secretary of State the power to extinguish or divert a path to enable a new road to be built.

The procedure to be followed for extinguishing or diverting paths under the Town and Country Planning Act, 1971 is the same as in Sections 110 and 111 of the Highways Act, 1959 outlined above.

Creation of Paths

Although England and Wales are blessed with a very dense network of footpaths and bridleways, it is sometimes necessary to create paths. The most usual cases are short stretches to link existing rights of way for long-distance paths and occasionally, where the changing pattern of land use makes it desirable, for a new path to be created either by agreement or order to link with existing paths and thus preserve the path network.

The authority making the creation agreement or order,

which may be a County Council, District Council or a National Park Board, must bear the following considerations in mind: (a) the extent to which the path would add to the convenience or enjoyment of a substantial section of the public, or to the convenience of local residents; (b) the effect the path will have on the rights of persons interested in the land.

As far as possible new paths are created by agreement and the number of creation orders is very small. Compensation must be paid to the landowner if a path is created.

If a path is created by order, the procedure for advertising and objecting is similar to that for extinguishing and diverting paths.

Waymarking and Signposting

Waymarking may be defined as marking the course of the route at points along it. Waymarking is complementary to signposting, which is normally reserved for the points where a path makes a junction with a road. Signposts advertise a path and its initial direction; waymarks enable users to follow the path accurately at points where they might otherwise have difficulty.

Under Section 27 of the Countryside Act, 1968, highway authorities have a statutory duty to signpost all paths where they leave a metalled road unless the Parish Council or chairman of the Parish Meeting is satisfied that a signpost is not necessary. Many people will be familiar with the green and white metal sign or the wooden finger post indicating a footpath or bridleway.

In April 1973, the Countryside Commission set up a study group to report on the need for and problems of waymarking in England and Wales and the policies and practices of different authorities and organizations in waymarking, and to make recommendations for a national code for waymarking. Their report was published by Her Majesty's Stationery Office in December 1974, and made the following recommendations:

(1) That the Department of the Environment should consider whether or not legislation is needed to clarify Section 27 of the Countryside Act, 1968 concerning the responsibilities and duties of local authorities to signpost and waymark public footpaths and bridleways.

(2) That the Department consider whether or not legislation is needed to rectify the present position whereby there is no general definition of the width of a public footpath or bridleway. This should be considered especially in relation to new public paths and the diversion of existing paths.

(3) That public footpaths and bridleways in England and Wales should be waymarked at all points where the appropriate local or National Park Authority consider waymarking necessary.

(4) That the criterion which local authorities should adopt in deciding where, if any, waymarking is necessary on a particular footpath or bridleway should be whether or not a stranger would have difficulty in following the course of the path if the route were not marked. (An exception to this principle, in relation to mountain areas and moorland country, is suggested.)

(5) That a basic symbol should be adopted for use on public paths where waymarking is carried out but that the materials to be used and the methods to be followed in applying the waymark should have regard to local terrain and available surfaces.

(6) That footpaths and bridleways should be distinguished from one another by the use of a different colour for each of the two categories of path.

(7) That the definition of the waymark should be as follows:
  (a) *Shape:* An arrow of the shape illustrated in Figure 25
  (b) *Colours:* Footpaths – Yellow 08 E 51 (British Standard range 4800)
    Bridleways – Blue 20 E 51 (British Standard range 4800)

(8) That the height from the ground at which the waymark should normally be placed is similar for both footpaths

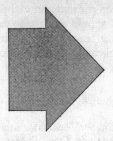

Fig. 25 The waymark symbol

and bridleways. The height recommended for general use is
eye-level, approximately 1·5 metres.

(9) That all local authorities and others responsible for
work on public rights of way should recognize their responsibility to signpost and waymark public paths to the extent
that any visitors who are unfamiliar with the area will not
lose their way. Provision should be made for this work to be
done, including the allocation of adequate financial and
staff resources.

(10) That local authorities should regard the waymarking
of public paths as making an important contribution towards the improvement of recreation opportunities in the
countryside.

(11) That local authorities, in considering proposals for
waymarking schemes, should seek to secure by the fullest
possible consultation the co-operation of those landowners
and farmers affected, allowing adequate opportunity for
alternative siting to be made by those whose land is crossed
by public rights of way which it is proposed to waymark.

(12) That local authorities should encourage and co-
operate with responsible voluntary organizations and individuals in the implementation and maintenance of
well-conceived waymarking schemes and the publication of
maps and guides; that they should provide for them the
necessary materials and assistance.

(13) That where waymarking has been undertaken the
authorities should give wide publicity to the waymarked

paths in their respective areas and to the waymarking system itself, and that they should encourage the display of maps of public rights of way near the footpaths and at prominent places, including libraries, council offices, parish halls and church porches.

Bibliography

CAMPBELL, IAN, *A Practical Guide to the Law of Footpaths and Bridle-ways*, 4th edn, Commons, Open Spaces and Footpath Preservation Society, 166 Shaftesbury Avenue, London WC2, 1974.

MCAREVEY, MARY, *A Guide to Definitive Maps of Public Paths*, 3rd edn, Commons, Open Spaces and Footpaths Preservation Society, 1974.

9   THE LAW RELATING TO FOOTPATHS AND BRIDLEWAYS IN ENGLAND AND WALES

It is surprising how little even keen walkers know of the law relating to public paths. Most motorists have at least a working knowledge of their rights and statutory obligations. If users of public paths took the trouble to master the main outline of path law, they would have much greater confidence in dealing with problems and perhaps there would be fewer attempts deliberately to obstruct paths and the path network would be much better used. It is not generally realized that public paths have much the same protection in law as trunk roads, and the term 'highway' when used without qualification in an Act of Parliament includes all routes over which the public may lawfully pass, be they trunk roads or paths. It is as much an offence to obstruct a classified road with barbed wire as it is to erect a fence across a public path without giving proper access, and the penalty for doing so is exactly the same. The most important statutes dealing with public paths are:

National Parks and Access to the Countryside Act, 1949
Highways Act, 1959
Countryside Act, 1968
Highways Act, 1971

In addition, there are numerous other Acts which affect paths but which are comparatively rarely used, although of course when applied they may have important consequences locally.

In one chapter it is not possible to do more than outline the main provisions of the law and all path users are urged to obtain a copy of the book by Ian Campbell mentioned in the bibliography at the end of this chapter. This is a remarkably lucid and entertaining guide to path law written for the layman by an expert.

Outline of Path Law

(1) *Definitions*

(a) Footpath: A footpath is a highway over which the public have right of way on foot only.

(b) Bridleway: A bridleway is a highway over which the public have right of way on foot, on horseback and on a pedal bicycle.

(c) Road used as public path: A RUPP is a highway other than a public path used by the public mainly for the purpose for which footpaths or bridleways are so used. Under the Countryside Act, 1968, all RUPPs are to be reclassified as either byways, open to all traffic, bridleways or footpaths.

(d) Byways: A byway is a very minor road, usually unmetalled, that is nevertheless open to all traffic.

(2) *Rights of Way Maps* County Councils have a statutory duty to prepare Definitive Maps of footpaths and bridleways. If a footpath or bridleway appears on the Definitive Map, that is conclusive evidence in law of the existence of a right of way unless an extinguishment or diversion has been granted by due legal process (see Chapter 8). If a path has been included in the Definitive Map by mistake it remains a right of way until the error is corrected by the publication of the next revised Definitive Map.

(3) *Gates and Stiles* Landowners have a legal duty to maintain in good condition all gates and stiles crossed by public footpaths and bridleways. The highway authority is under an obligation to contribute at least 25 per cent of the approved cost of the work. If the work is not done, the highway authority can do what is necessary and charge the cost to the landowner. All gates on bridleways must be capable of being

opened by a rider without dismounting and stiles must not be built across bridleways. (Countryside Act, 1968, Section 28.)

(4) *Obstructions* Landowners are required to keep public footpaths and bridleways free of obstructions such as overgrown hedges, barbed wire, crops etc. Failure to do so carries a maximum penalty of £50. (Highways Act, 1959, Section 121.)

(5) *Ploughing* Under the Highways Act, 1959, Section 119, as amended by the Countryside Act, 1968, Section 29, a farmer may plough a public path or bridleway which crosses a field in the interests of good husbandry. If he decides to plough a public path or bridleway he is required to:

(a) give seven days' written notice of his intention to the County Council (failure to do so carries a maximum penalty of £10).

(b) restore the surface of the path or bridleway within six weeks of giving notice of ploughing (within three weeks if the County Council were not notified) so as to make it reasonably convenient for the exercise of the public right of way (failure to do so carries a maximum penalty of £50).

It is nearly always illegal to plough headland paths (i.e. paths that follow the edge of a field) although in some rare cases a common-law right to plough a headland path may exist. In any case, the onus of proof of such a right to plough is on the landowner.

Ploughing probably causes more ill-feeling than any other path problem. It is worth remembering that it is only since the war that farmers have had a general right to plough non-headland paths, and in many parts of the country they have now been ploughed so often that local people have given up trying to use them, for there are few more formidable obstacles than a large, wet, deep-ploughed field. There is a statutory duty to restore paths after they have been ploughed but this obligation is widely ignored. In the past two years I have surveyed every path in thirty-three parishes in north

Buckinghamshire and in none of them was there any evidence that a path had been restored. There was just one bridleway that was left with an unploughed strip in the middle of a large field. Where fields are very large, it is possible to leave the path unploughed, and the Chiltern Society has had considerable success in persuading farmers to adopt this method. However, with modern farming methods it is not practicable to do this in small fields.

Restoring the surface of the path is so easy! The practice recommended by the National Farmers' Union is for the ploughman to drive his tractor along the line of the path, turn it round, placing his offside rear wheel in the track it has already made, and drive along the path again. This makes an indentation not more than eighteen inches wide which clearly defines the line of the path. Ideally, the path should be defined after each stage of cultivation, namely ploughing, harrowing, drilling and rolling. Even though ripe corn may close over the path, the line will be quite clear and the walker will pass through the crop parting it as a ship cleaves the waves.

(6) *Footbridges* Under Section 294 of the Highways Act, 1959, the highway authority has a duty to maintain bridges. However, this obligation does not always apply, as in some cases another authority such as British Rail or British Waterways may be responsible for maintaining the bridge.

(7) *Dangerous Animals* Most County Councils have adopted a by-law prohibiting bulls over twelve months old running free in a field crossed by a public path, although some counties permit this if the bull is accompanied by cows. Although it is not an offence to have dangerous animals, other than bulls, in a field crossed by a public path the owner of the animal is liable for any damage or injury it may cause.

(8) *Misleading Notices* Under Section 57 of the National Parks and Access to the Countryside Act, 1949, it is an

offence to display a notice containing a misleading statement likely to deter the public from using a public path.
Thus it is an offence to erect a notice warning 'Beware of
the bull' if there is never a bull in that field. Notices such as
'Trespassers will be prosecuted' and 'Private road' are more
difficult to deal with. The walker who strays from the path *is*
trespassing and it is possible that it is a private road with a
right of way on foot over it. One possible solution is for the
County Council to erect a footpath signpost near the notice.

Enforcement of the Law

As can be seen from the above outline, much of the law
relating to public paths is clear, unambiguous and fairly
easily comprehended. Unfortunately, the mere existence of
a law does not carry the guarantee that it will be obeyed,
and there is no doubt that, in many parts of the country,
path law is largely ignored. How, then, can pressure be
brought to bear on those who are not carrying out their legal
obligations?

County Councils have a statutory duty to assert and protect the rights of those who use paths. A stranger or occasional visitor has little choice but to write to the County
Council concerned giving details of the problem quoting, if
possible, the parish and path number and certainly giving
the grid reference (see Chapter 5). Sooner or later, the
County Council will take some kind of action, but it must
be remembered that in most counties the paths section of the
Highways Department is likely to be very understaffed.

A local person can do a lot more, and there are several
lines of action which can be taken. If a farmer or landowner
is at fault, he can be approached direct by telephone or
letter. If it is not known to whom the land belongs an in-
telligent guess can be made by relating gates and farm tracks
to a particular farm and establishing the name of the farm
from the map. The local public library will provide you with
the name of the occupier of the farm from the Electoral Roll.
A polite and carefully worded letter or telephone call sug-

gesting that the problem may be on their land will often produce results. Parish Councils can also be very helpful. The name of the Parish Clerk can be obtained from the public library or the Chief Executive of the District Council. Many Parish Councils are very jealous of their local paths and can often get results quickly.

Private Prosecutions

The local rambling club or footpaths society will probably take the matter up for you, as may the local office of the National Farmers' Union, but if all else fails there are legal remedies. In my view, these should be used only as a last resort and only after repeated efforts have failed to produce results. It is much better to use persuasion rather than totally alienate the local farming community by rushing into hasty legal action. Nevertheless, someone may prove to be recalcitrant, in which case the only remedy will be to invoke the law.

The citizen, either as an individual or on behalf of an organization, can invoke Section 59 of the Highways Act, 1959 to compel the highway authority to repair a highway. The first thing that has to be done is to establish from the Chief Executive of the County Council whether they admit responsibility for the highway. If responsibility is admitted, but nothing is done, it is possible to get an order from the magistrate's court compelling the authority to carry out the necessary work. This tactic is extremely useful in the case of missing footbridges and for minor obstructions.

If a local authority is clearly in breach of its statutory obligation under the Highways Act, 1959 'to assert and protect the rights of the public to the use and enjoyment of all highways and to prevent, as far as possible, the stopping up or obstruction of those highways', then the local Ombudsman may be able to help. In 1975 the Wigan Footpath Society laid a complaint of maladministration against the St Helen's Metropolitan District Council on the grounds that the local authority had taken little or no action to get obstructions removed from four footpaths. The complaint was upheld and, although the local Ombudsman has no powers to force an authority to act, his opinion is likely to carry great weight.

The procedure for approaching the Ombudsman is set out in the booklet *Your Local Ombudsman* which may be seen at most local libraries or obtained from The Commission for Local Administration in England, 21 Queen Anne's Gate, London SW1H 9BU.

An individual can prosecute for obstruction under Section 121 of the Highways Act, 1959: 'If a person, without lawful authority or excuse, in any way wilfully obstructs the free passage along a highway he shall be guilty of an offence and shall be liable in respect thereof to a fine not exceeding fifty pounds.' This is particularly useful for dealing with problems like barbed wire and hedges with no access through them. Obtain from the Clerk of the Justices Form No. 1 as prescribed by the Magistrates Courts (Forms) Rules, 1968. The form should be completed in simple language naming the person concerned who has caused the obstruction on path number — contrary to Section 121 of the Highways Act, 1959. The Justices Clerk will then issue a summons to the defendant. At the hearing, the complainant must produce a copy of the Definitive Map certified by the highway authority that no extinguishment or diversion has been granted.

An individual may take certain steps to remove physically an obstruction on a path providing that he is on a *bona fide* journey and not setting out with the sole intention of removing the obstruction and also providing that only enough of the obstruction is removed to allow free passage along the path. Great caution should be used in removing obstructions for, if stock strays or becomes infected from neighbouring animals, it may result in thousands of pounds' worth of damage. It is probably kinder to initiate a private prosecution if persuasion fails to have the obstacle removed and the resulting publicity in the local press may have a salutary effect.

Improvement of Paths

If there are many path problems in your area and no organization for their protection exists, you might consider forming one. Such organizations take many forms. They may be rambling clubs, riding clubs (whose members are likely to be interested only in bridleways) or rights of way societies which can bring riders and walkers together for their mutual benefit. A letter to the local paper announcing a public meeting to discuss path problems is likely to bring a surprisingly large audience and often representatives from the highway authority will attend, if invited, and answer questions. An active society can in three or four years improve the condition of local paths and people will find that they are usable again.

Many Parish Councils hold an annual walk of all the paths in their parish. Unfortunately, they do not always take up the problems they discover with the landowner or relevant authority. If your Parish Council does not walk its paths, encourage them to do so and, if necessary, offer to lead them and try to ensure that the Parish Clerk takes any necessary remedial action.

A local rambling club or rights of way society can improve local paths by bridging ditches and clearing excessive growth. Officials of the highway authority will often be only too pleased to supply materials such as old railway sleepers and deliver them to the site. They will negotiate with the landowner for permission to erect bridges and agree on the exact line of the path so that vegetation can be removed.

Ditches up to about twelve feet wide are best bridged with old railway sleepers. Carefully measure the length of the sleeper required and the highway authority will have them cut to size and delivered as close to the site as they can get a vehicle. A twelve-foot sleeper can be carried for half a mile or so by four men taking the weight on two lengths of iron piping. If the ditch is not liable to flood, the bank should be dug out so that the sleeper lies flush to the surface. Wooden pegs hammered into the ground on each side of the sleeper and then nailed to it will hold it in position (Figure 26). For lengths over six feet, it is better to use two sleepers side by side.

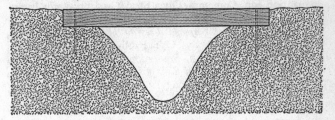

Fig. 26 Ditch-bridging

For clearing undergrowth from the surface of a path the following equipment will be found useful:

billhooks
slashers
toggle-loppers (fearsome secateurs with 18-ins. handles which will remove branches 2 ins. thick with one snip)
axes
saws
secateurs

Remove from the line of the path all vegetation including saplings and any branches hanging over the path less than seven feet from the ground. It is as well to agree beforehand with the landowner about the disposal of hedge trimmings. He may want them burnt in a special area or he may prefer them to be heaped at intervals and allowed to rot. Under no circumstances allow them to fall into ditches as they will block them and may cause flooding.

Many highway authorities are prepared to make token payments to club funds for work of this kind. Do not hesitate to ask, for you are saving the ratepayers' money by doing the work of the highway authority for them.

Bibliography

CAMPBELL, IAN, *A Practical Guide to the Law of Footpaths and Bridle-ways*, 4th edn, Commons, Open Spaces and Footpaths Preservation Society, 166 Shaftesbury Avenue, London WC2, 1974.

GARNER, J., *Rights of Way and Access to the Countryside*, 3rd edn, Oyez Practice Notes No. 55, Oyez Publishing, 1974.

RAMBLERS' ASSOCIATION, *Private Prosecutions in the Magistrates Court for Obstruction of Public Right of Way*, Rambler's Association, 1–4 Crawford Mews, London WIH IPT, 1975.

The world's first national park was the Yellowstone Park in the USA, which was established in 1872 by an Act of Congress. In 1889, there was a farsighted leader in the *Manchester Guardian* which suggested that the Lake District should be nationalized or, failing that, some kind of conservation should be adopted to prevent spoliation of the area by commercial interests. During the next fifty years, a movement developed to gain more public access to mountains, and Bills were introduced in Parliament in 1908, 1924, 1926 and 1927 in an attempt to achieve this end. For various reasons they were not successful and in 1932 a mass trespass took place on Kinder Scout. Fighting took place between gamekeepers and walkers, the police stepped in and a number of arrests were made. The local magistrates handed out some savage prison sentences, but the honesty, integrity and above all the gentleness of those who suffered for their obvious love of the mountains caught the public imagination and by 1939 the Access to the Mountains Act became law.

During the war a number of committees sat and reports were commissioned that resulted in significant social changes in the post-war years. Some, like the Beveridge Report, have radically changed our lives; others are not so well known to the public but have nevertheless improved the quality of our lives. Into the latter category falls a report by a committee presided over by Lord Justice Scott which stated in 1942 that 'the establishment of national parks in Britain is long overdue'. In 1943 the new Ministry of Town and Country Planning was formed and one of the Minister's first acts was to ask an architect, John Dower, to write a report on the problems involved in setting up national parks. John Dower defined a national park as 'an extensive area of beautiful and relatively wild country in which, for the nation's benefit and by appropriate national decision and action, (a) the characteristic landscape beauty is strictly preserved; (b) access and facilities for public open air enjoyment are amply provided; (c) wildlife and buildings and places of architectural and historic interest are suitably protected, while (d) established farming area is effectively maintained.'

The minister set up a new Committee in 1945 under Sir Arthur Hobhouse to consider the Dower proposals and recommended that national parks should be set up in the following areas:

Brecon Beacons
Dartmoor
Exmoor
Lake District
North York Moors
Northumberland
Peak District
Pembrokeshire Coast
Snowdonia
Yorkshire Dales
The South Downs
The Norfolk Broads

All these areas have now achieved the status of national parks except the South Downs and the Norfolk Broads. The Hobhouse Committee drew up a list of regions of outstanding landscape value deserving of being conservation areas which have formed the basis of the programme for Areas of Outstanding Natural Beauty.

It should be noted that in British national parks there is normally no change in the ownership of the land. The nation does not own its national parks, as some countries do, so the right of access for walkers, riders and others using them for recreation is no greater than in other parts of the country unless local arrangements have been negotiated.

Each national park is administered by an executive committee made up of representatives from interested organizations such as County Councils, and has its own national park officer who is responsible to the executive committee. Most of the funds for national parks come from central government and are used for providing such things as car parks, toilets, picnic areas, camp sites, footpaths, bridleways and nature trails, information centres, publicity and warden services. The executive committee is also the planning authority and keeps a very tight control on all development to ensure that it fits in with the traditional style of building of the area. Any industrial development has to be properly screened and made as unobtrusive as possible.

One of the criteria for selecting areas for national parks is that they should contain a high proportion of open country, which is defined in the National Parks and Access to the Countryside Act, 1949 as 'mountain, moor, heath, down, cliff or foreshore' and excludes agricultural land except rough grazing for sheep and cattle. Thus national parks are particularly suitable for walking holidays. Much of the terrain is rugged and must be treated by the novice with great caution. Many national parks organize walks led by experienced walkers with the aim of introducing people to the pleasures of upland walking. For those who do not wish to venture into the moors and mountains, there are numerous delightful walks to be taken in the valleys of the national parks.

Bibliography

BELL, MERVYN, editor, *Britain's National Parks*, David & Charles, 1975.

BUSH, ROGER, *The National Parks of England and Wales together with Areas of Outstanding Natural Beauty and Long Distance Footpaths and Bridleways*, Dent, 1973.

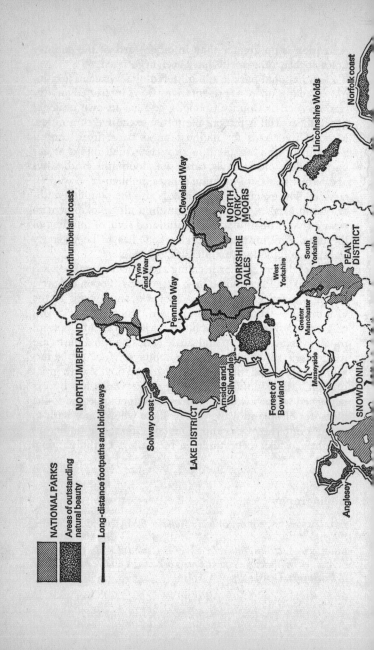

NATIONAL PARKS

Areas of outstanding natural beauty

Long-distance footpaths and bridleways

Northumberland coast

NORTHUMBERLAND

Solway coast

LAKE DISTRICT

Pennine Way

Arnside and Silverdale

Forest of Bowland

SNOWDONIA

Anglesey

Cleveland Way

NORTH YORK MOORS

YORKSHIRE DALES

Tyne and Wear

West Yorkshire

Greater Manchester

Merseyside

South Yorkshire

PEAK DISTRICT

Lincolnshire Wolds

Norfolk coast

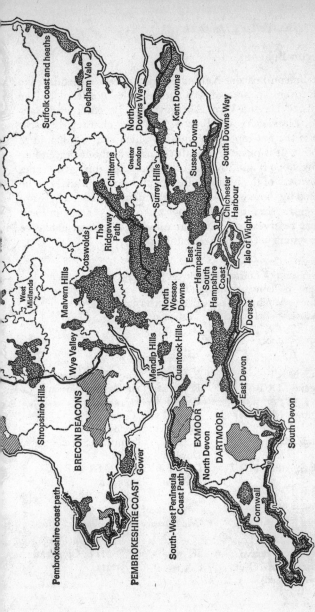

Fig. 27 National Parks, Areas of Outstanding Natural Beauty, Long-Distance Footpaths and Bridleways

Brecon Beacons

The Brecon Beacons National Park was established in 1957 and covers an area of 519 square miles bordered by the towns of Hay-on-Wye, Abergavenny, Brynamman, Llandeilo, Llandovery and Brecon. The most characteristic feature is the flat-topped mountains which rise to a height of 2,906 ft. It is possible to walk for miles without descending below 2,000 ft and, by way of contrast, the thirty-two miles of towpath of the Monmouthshire and Brecon Canal can be walked by those who fancy less strenuous exercise. There are numerous sites of archaeological interest, three national nature reserves and, at Agen Allwedd, the most extensive cave system yet discovered in this country.

Information Centres
Abergavenny – Lower Monk Street (Tel. 3254)
Brecon – 6 Glamorgan Street (Tel. 2763)
Libanus – Mountain Centre (Tel. Brecon 3366)
Llandovery – 8 Broad Street (Tel. 20693)

RESCUE TEAMS

Name	*Hon. Secretary*
Brecon MRT	E. Bartlett, Tyn-y-Caeau, Brecon
Bridgend MRT	R. Ramsay, 34a Oakfield Street, Cardiff
Longtown MRT	J. Van Laun, Court House, Longtown, Herefordshire
Morlais MRT	C. Davis, 15 Bryntirion Street, Dowlais
RAF St Athan MRT	Officer in Charge, MRT, RAF St Athan, Glamorgan

MANNED POSTS

Location	*Grid Reference*	*Telephone*
1–10 Powell Street, Penwyllt, Abercrave, Swansea Valley. (Not always manned)	SN 855 155	Abercrave 613 or 211 or Glynneath 211

Location	Grid Reference	Telephone
Youth Adventure Centre, Longtown, Herefordshire	SO 322 291	Longtown Castle 225
Swindon Outdoor Centre, Plas Pencelli, Brecon	SO 091 248	Llanfrynach 241
Dolygaer Outdoor Pursuits Centre, Dolygaer, Merthyr Tydfil	SO 060 145	Merthyr Tydfil 5305
Cardiff Youth Adventure Centre, Storey Arms, Libanus	SO 983 204	Brecon 3598

For rescue go to the rescue post or telephone, whichever is quicker. Dial 999, ask for the police. The position of a post is somemes changed. Verify locally.

Maps

1:50000 sheets 159, 160, 161
1:25000 Brecon Beacons Outdoor Leisure maps (3 sheets)

Guidebook

DAVIES, MARGARET, editor, *Brecon Beacons National Park,* HMSO, 1967.

Footpath Guides

BARBER, CHRISTOPHER, *Walks in the Brecon Beacons*, Pridgeon Publishing Ltd, 1976.

POUCHER, W. A., *The Welsh Peaks: A Pictorial Guide to Walking in this Region and to the Safe Ascent of its Principal Mountain Groups*, 5th edn, Constable, 1973.

WESTACOTT, H. D., *Walks and Rides in the Brecon Beacons*, Footpath Publications, Adstock Cottage, Adstock, Buckingham, 1977.

Dartmoor

Dartmoor National Park covers an area of 365 square miles in central and south Devonshire between Exeter and Plymouth. It was established in 1951 and is the only piece of really wild country left in southern England. Much of

Dartmoor lies between 1,000 and 1,500 ft above sea level, with High Willhays reaching 2,038 ft. Its many outcrops of granite have been eroded by the wind into strange shapes and in some places the huge granite blocks have been shattered into 'clitters' by the action of snow and ice.

On a warm summer's day with the roads jammed with holidaymakers' cars it is difficult to imagine the very real dangers of Dartmoor. But the paths and tracks over the moors are not always clearly defined and there are large areas of deep and treacherous bog. Moreover, mists can come in very quickly from the sea and catch the unwary, and this can be a very frightening experience. Unfortunately, the army uses a large part of the northern side of the moor for training exercises and artillery practice; information about dates and times of firing can be obtained from local post offices. Red flags are flown when firing is taking place.

Dartmoor is a natural outdoor museum containing numerous hut circles, stone circles, cairns, tumuli, hill forts and clapper bridges.

Information Centre
Two Bridges – (caravan – summer months only)
(Tel. Princetown 253)

RESCUE TEAMS

Name	*Hon. Secretary*
Dartmoor Rescue Group – teams from Plymouth, Tavistock and Okehampton	W. H. D. Ames, Court Gate, Tavistock

MANNED POST

Location	*Grid Reference*
Police Station, Guildhall Square, Tavistock	SX 483 745

UNMANNED POSTS

Dewarstone Rock, River Plym, SW Dartmoor. (Stretcher only – not manned, no phone)	SX 533 635	The stretcher is attached to the wall of Endomoor Cottage

All calls for rescue must be made to the police, dialling 999.

Maps
1 :63360 Tourist map of Dartmoor
1 :50000 sheets 191, 201, 202
1 :25000 sheets SX55, SX65, SX75, SX46, SX56, SX66, SX76, SX47, SX57, SX67, SX77, SX87, SX48, SX58, SX68, SX78, SX88, SX59, SX69, SX79, SX89

Guidebook
HOSKINS, W. G., *Dartmoor National Park*, HMSO, 1972.

Footpath Guides
CROSSING, WILLIAM, *Guide to Dartmoor* (1909), David & Charles, 1974.
WESTACOTT, H. D., *Walks and Rides on Dartmoor*, Footpath Publications, Adstock Cottage, Adstock, Buckingham, 1977.

Exmoor

Exmoor National Park is the second smallest national park in England. It covers 265 square miles and was established in 1954. It stretches along the coast from Combe Martin to Minehead and goes inland as far as Dulverton. The scenery is mostly moorland intersected by deep wooded valleys known as combes and, of course, there are some magnificent cliffs along the coast. The highest point is Dunkery Beacon (1,705 ft) but much of Exmoor lies between 1,000 and 1,500 ft. Exmoor probably offers some of the easiest walking in any of the National Parks and, like Dartmoor, there are numerous prehistoric remains.

Information Centres
Combe Martin – Beach Carpark (caravan – summer months only) (Tel. 3319)

Dulverton – Exmoor House (Tel. 665)
Lynmouth – Parish Hall
Minehead – Market House, The Parade (Tel. 2984)

Rescue Post
None. Dial 999 and ask for rescue service.

Maps
1:63360 Tourist map of Exmoor
1:50000 sheets 180, 181
1:25000 sheets SS72, SS82, SS92, SS63, SS73, SS83, SS93, SS54, SS64, SS74, SS84, SS94, SS75, ST03, ST04

Guidebook
COLEMAN-COOKE, JOHN, editor, *Exmoor National Park*, HMSO, 1972.

Footpath Guides
ABBOT, TIM, *Exmoor Coastal Walks*, 2nd edn, Cider Press, Hillside, Church Path, Minehead, 1975.
ABBOT, TIM, *Exmoor Walks*, 3rd edn, Cider Press, Hillside, Church Path, Minehead, 1974.
SOMERSET COUNTY COUNCIL, *Exmoor National Park: Waymarked Walks 1* and *Waymarked Walks 2*, 3rd edns, County Planning Department, 1972.

Lake District

The Lake District National Park is the largest of them all, covering an area of 866 square miles. It is roughly square in shape and is bordered by the towns of Penrith and Cockermouth in the north and Millom and Kendal in the south. The Lake District's unique beauty lies in the combination of steep sided mountains interspersed by numerous lakes. As the area is so near the sea, the mountains appear higher than they actually are because they rise so dramatically from the low ground. The natural beauty of the Lake District is enhanced by its beautiful, if humble, stone buildings. The larger towns of the Lake District – Keswick, Ambleside and Windermere – can be horribly crowded in high summer but there are some quiet hamlets and villages and, providing the more popular walks are avoided, it is still possible to be alone in the mountains.

Information Centres
Ambleside – Old Court House, Church Street (Tel. 3084)
Bowness – Bowness Bay, Glebe Road (Tel. Windermere 2895)
Brockhole – National Park Centre, Windermere (Tel.2231) – day visitor centre only
Hawkshead (caravan) – Car Park, Ambleside
Windermere – Bank House, High Street (Tel. 2498) – no personal callers – Mobile

RESCUE TEAMS

Name	*Hon. Secretary*
Keswick MRT	John Wood, Rowling End, Millbeck, Keswick
Coniston MRT	Rev. J. C. Hancock, The Vicarage, Coniston
Outward Bound Mountain School, Eskdale	The Warden
Outward Bound Mountain School, Ullswater	The Warden
Cockermouth MRT	Paul D. Horder, 46 Towers Lane, Cockermouth
Langdale and Ambleside MRT	Dr D. Earnshaw, Glenridding House, Stoney Lane, Ambleside
Kendal Mountain Search and Rescue Team	P. Rogers, 6 Greengate, Levens, nr Kendal, LA8 8NF
Penrith MRT	F. W. Matthews, Meadowbank, Kings Meaburn, Penrith, Cumbria
Patterdale MRT	B. Spurrett, Aira Cottage, Dockray, nr Penrith, Cumbria
Wasdale MRT	M. Pringle, 42 Coniston Avenue, Seascale, Cumbria
Millom Fell Rescue Team	J. Mitchell, 26 Pannatt Hill, Millom
Kirkby Stephen Fell Search Team	Peter Day, Thorne Mount, South Road, Kirkby Stephen

Name	Hon. Secretary
Sedbergh Fell Rescue Team	Bryan Hinton, Farfield, Sedbergh
RAF Leeming MRT	Officer in Charge, MRT, RAF Leeming, Northallerton, Yorks
Search Dogs Organizer, Search and Rescue Dog Association	G. E. Reid, 1 Millbank Cottages, Keswick, Cumbria

RESCUE POSTS, Manned, with Telephone

Location	Grid Reference	Telephone
Wasdale, Wastwater Hotel	NY 187 088	Wasdale 229
Borrowdale, Seathwaite Farm, Seathwaite	NY 236 121	Borrowdale 284
Keswick Police Station	NY 266 236	Keswick 72004
Ennerdale Youth Hostel. (Emergency phone to police only – not manned)	NY 142 141	
Dungeon Ghyll, Old Hotel, Great Langdale	NY 286 061	Langdale 272
Sub-Post, Police House, Grasmere		
Sun Hotel, Coniston	SD 300 976	Coniston 248
Buttermere, Gatesgarth Farm	NY 194 149	Buttermere 256
Eskdale, Outward Bound School	NY 143 002	Eskdale 281
Patterdale Youth Hostel, Goldrill	NY 399 156	Glenridding 394
Ullswater, Outward Bound School	NY 438 213	Pooley Bridge 347
Moor Road, Millom	SD 169 802	Millom 2207

Location	Grid Reference	Telephone
Cumbria CC Ambulance Service Depot, Bainbridge Road, Sedbergh	SD 656 922	Sedbergh 20595

Unmanned Posts

Pillar Rock (40 yds E of Walkers Gully)	NY 172 124	
Dow Crag (at foot of Abrahams B Buttress)	SD 264 976	
Mickledore, Scafell (just below crest Eskdale Side)	NY 210 068	
Sty Head Pass	NY 218 095	
The Knott, High Street	NY 438 127	
The Fisher Stretcher Box, Striding Edge	NY 359 156	

The Lake District Mountain Accidents Association consists of the teams listed together with many others on call through the police. Its Hon. Secretary is E. C. Downham, The Maisonette, Compston Road, Ambleside, Cumbria. Tel. Ambleside 2297.

Search and rescue operations are organized and directed by its Advisory Panel in co-operation with the police (Hon. Secretary, Chief Supt. R. J. Willat, Cumbria Constabulary HQ, Carleton Hall, Penrith. Tel. Penrith 4411).

For rescue go to rescue post or telephone, whichever is quicker. Dial 999, ask for the police. The position of a post is sometimes changed.

Verify locally.

Maps
1:63360 Tourist map of the Lake District
1:50000 sheets 85, 89, 90, 96, 97
1:25000 Outdoor Leisure map (4 sheets)

Guidebook
PEARSALL, W. H., *The Lake District National Park*, HMSO, 1969

Footpath Guides
There are many footpath guides to the Lake District. The best is:

WAINWRIGHT, ALFRED W., *A Pictorial Guide to the Lakeland Fells*,
Westmorland Gazette: Vol. 1 Eastern Fells; Vol. 2 Far Eastern
Fells; Vol. 3 Central Fells; Vol. 4 Southern Fells; Vol. 5 North-
ern Fells; Vol. 6 North-Western Fells; Vol. 7 Western Fells.

The following are also useful:

PARKER, JOHN, *Lake District Walks for Motorists*, Gerrard Publications: *Central Area*, 1971; *Northern Area: Keswick, Borrowdale
and Ullswater*, 2nd edn, 1974; *Western Area: Buttermere, Wastwater,
Eskdale West of Coniston and to the Coast*, 1974.
POUCHER, W. A., *The Lakeland Peaks: A Pictorial Guide to Walking
in the District and to the Safe Ascent of its Principal Mountain Groups*,
5th edn, Constable, 1971.

North York Moors

The North York Moors National Park covers an area of
553 square miles bordered by the towns of Saltburn, Scarborough, Helmsley and Northallerton. It is the largest
heather moor in England and in August when the heather
is in flower it is a marvellous sight. Another feature of this
national park is the magnificent cliff scenery, which includes
Robin Hood's Bay and the beautiful fishing village of
Staithes. The moors are littered with reminders of prehistoric man and there are a number of fine medieval
crosses. By contrast, the huge, weird concrete domes of the
early-warning radar system are situated on Fylingdales
Moor.

Information Centres
Danby – Danby Lodge National Park Centre, near Whitby (Tel.
Castleton 654) – day visitor centre only
Sutton Bank – Information Centre, top of Sutton Bank by the
A170 – personal callers only
Mobiles (2)

RESCUE TEAM

Name	*Hon. Secretary*
Scarborough and District Search and Rescue Team	Mrs J. A. E. Gough, Heather Croft, Ravenscar, Scarborough

MANNED POST

Location	Grid Reference	Telephone
2 Mount Pleasant, Scalby, Scarborough	TA 010 905	Scarborough 72530

For rescue go to the rescue post or telephone, whichever is quicker. Dial 999, ask for police. The position of a post is sometimes changed. Verify locally.

Guidebook

RAISTRICK, ARTHUR, editor, *The North York Moors National Park*, HMSO, 1971.

Maps

1:63360 Tourist map of the North York Moors

1:50000 sheets 93, 94, 99, 100, 101

1:25000 sheets SE57, SE67, SE48, SE58, SE68, SE78, SE88, SE98, SE49, SE59, SE69, SE79, SE89, SE99, NZ40, NZ50, NZ60, NZ70, NZ80, NZ90, NZ51, NZ61, NZ71, NZ81, NZ91, TA08, TA09

Footpath Guides

BALMAIN, WADE, *Greentracks and Heather Tracks*, Vol 2, H.O. Wade, 5 Eastview, Highfields, Rowlands Gill, Tyne and Wear, 1976.

FALCONER, A. A., *Walking in Cleveland: 28 Walks in North Yorkshire*, Dalesman, 1968.

RAMBLERS' ASSOCIATION, *Walking on the North York Moors*, Dalesman, 1975.

WHITE, GEOFFREY, *North York Moors Walks for Motorists*. Gerrard Publications: *West and South – Hambledon Hills, Western Cleveland, Rydale, Bilsdale, Bransdale, Farndale and Rosedale*, 1973; *North and East – Cleveland Hills, Eskdale, Goathland, Newton Dale, Fylingdales Moor, Forests and Coasts*, 1974.

Northumberland

The Northumberland National Park is a long narrow one of 398 square miles stretching from just west of Hexham to the Scottish border. The park includes the Cheviot, rising to a height of 2,676 ft, and the best-preserved section of Hadrian's Wall. A visit to the Wall is a remarkable experience which demonstrates the might, power and orderliness of the Romans. Walkers have numerous routes from which to choose and, traditionally, access has always been permitted providing game and livestock are not disturbed.

Information Centres
Byrness – 9 Otterburn Green (Tel. Otterburn 622)
Ingram – Old School House (Tel. Powburn 248)
Once Brewed – Military Road, Hexham (Tel. Bardon Mill 396)
Rothbury – Church House, Church Street
Mobile

RESCUE TEAMS

Name	Hon. Secretary
Northumberland Wardens Fell Search and Rescue Team	M. H. Sawdon, 13 St George Road, Hexham, Northumberland
Northumberland LEA Mountain Activities Association Search and Rescue Team	J. L. Wainwright, 7 Western Avenue, Prudhoe, Northumberland
Upper Teasdale and Weardale Fell Rescue Association	D. Thompson, 5 Maughan Street, Shildon, Co. Durham
Cleveland Search and Rescue Team	B. A. Snowden, Weavers Cottage, Great Broughton, Middlesborough
RAF Leeming MRT	Officer in Charge, MRT, RAF Leeming, Northallerton, Yorks

SEARCH DOGS

Search and Rescue Dog Association (England)	K. G. Saxby, County Police Station, Mickleton, Barnard Castle, Co. Durham DL12 0LL

MANNED POSTS

Location	Grid Reference	Telephone
Police Station, Hexham	NY 929 639	Hexham 4111

Location	Grid Reference	Telephone
Ingram National Park Information Centre	NU 020 163	Powburn 248
Police Station, Yetholm, Kelso	NT 820 282	Kelso 42
High Force Hotel, Forest-in-Teasdale	NY 885 287	Forest-in-Teasdale 264
Glenwhelt, Westgate, Weardale	NY 902 373	Eastgate 227
Catton Field Study and Expedition Centre	NY 827 578	Allendale 327
Kielder Field Study and Expedition Centre	NY 633 919	Kielder 231
Howtel Mindrum Field Study and Expedition Centre	NT 892 334	Mindrum 239
Wauchope Field Study and Expedition Centre	NT 583 084	Bonchester Bridge 287

For rescue go to the rescue post or telephone whichever is quicker. Dial 999, ask for the police. The position of a post is sometimes changed. Verify locally.

Maps
1 :50000 sheets 74, 75, 80, 81, 86, 87
1 :25000 sheets NY66, NY76, NY86, NY67, NY77, NY87, NY68, NY78, NY88, NY79, NY89, NY99, NT60, NT70, NT80, NT90, NT71, NT81, NT91, NT82, NT92, NT83, NT93, NZ09, NU00, NU01, NU02

Guidebooks
PHILIPSON, JOHN, editor, *Northumberland National Park*, HMSO, 1969.

Footpath Guides
BALMAIN, WADE, *Green Tracks and Heather Tracks*, Vol. 1, H.O. Wade, 5 Eastview, Highfields, Rowlands Gill, Tyne and Wear, 1976.

W.H.–7

RAMBLERS' ASSOCIATION, *Ramblers' Cheviot: 12 Walks in the Cheviot Hills*, Harold Hill, 1969.

RAMBLERS' ASSOCIATION, *Ramblers' Tynedale: 10 Walks in the South West of Northumberland around Tyne, North Tyne and South Tyne Dales*, revised edn, Harold Hill, 1975.

Peak District

The Peak District National Park was the first National Park to be designated in Britain, and covers an area of 542 square miles bordered by the towns of Huddersfield, Sheffield, Ashbourne and Stockport. The southern part of the park is largely limestone and known as the White Peak, whereas the northern part is millstone grit and called the Dark Peak. The White Peak is gentler, greener and more cultivated than the Dark Peak, which is mountainous and contains a wilderness of groughs or peat bogs which seem to stretch for miles. The Kinder plateau (2,088 ft) is the highest point and is a stern test for walkers. There are numerous caverns in the Castleton area which can be visited. Some villages still keep up the old custom of 'well-dressing', when the wells are decorated with flowers to illustrate a bible story. Access agreements have been negotiated with some landowners, but parts of these moors may be closed during the shooting season. Notices giving details of closures are posted.

Information Centres
Bakewell – Market Hall, Bridge Street (Tel. 3227)
Buxton – St Ann's Well, The Crescent (Tel. 5106)
Castleton – Castle Street (Tel. Hope Valley 20679)
Dovestones – Dovestones Reservoir, near Greenfield – Sundays only

RESCUE TEAMS

Name	Hon. Secretary
Buxton MRT	Miss A. Knisely, Flat 2a, 9 Devonshire Road, Buxton, Derbyshire
Derby MRT	J. Tomlinson, Duffield Garage, Town Street, Duffield, Derbyshire

Name	*Hon. Secretary*
Edale MRT	P. A. Jackson, 9 King Edward Avenue, Glossop, Derbyshire
Glossop MRT	S. Fairhurst, 1 Farndon Drive, Timperley, Altrincham, Cheshire
Oldham MRT	P. J. Hyde, 7 School Street, Oldham, Lancs, OL8 1SE
Kinder MRT	Mrs J. Barnes, 6 The Birches, Hayfield, nr Stockport, Cheshire
Woodhead MRT	S. Marsden, 30 Lee Avenue, Deepcar, nr Sheffield
RAF Stafford MRT	Officer in Charge, MRT, Royal Air Force, Stafford

MANNED POSTS

Location	*Grid Reference*	*Telephone*
Warden Briefing Centre, Dovestones Dam	SE 013 034	Saddleworth 2075
Crowden Hostel	SK 073 993	Glossop 2135
Glossop Police Station	SK 036 942	Glossop 3141
Hayfield, Kinder Reservoir Filter Plant (N-W side of valley; 0700 – 1900 hours only)	SK 053 881	New Mills 43117
Information Centre, Edale	SK 124 856	Edale 216
Buxton Police Station, Silverlands (cave rescue equipment)	SK 063 734	Buxton 2811
White Hall Centre, Long Hill, nr Buxton	SK 032 763	Buxton 3260
Sub-Post, Warden Briefing Centre, Stoney Middleton	SK 232 753	Grindleford 30541
Matlock Police Station, Bank Road	SK 300 604	Matlock 3215

Location	Grid Reference

UNMANNED POSTS

Ranger Briefing Centre,   SK
Hollin Bank, Stanage.   238 836
(Break glass for key to
equipment store)

For rescue go to rescue post or telephone, whichever is quicker. Ring direct to the police operations room, Ripley 3551, or dial 999, asking for the police.

Maps

1:63360 Tourist map of the Peak District
1:50000 sheets 109, 110, 118, 119
1:25000 Outdoor Leisure map of the Dark Peak (covers most of the National Park north of a line from Bradwell to Chapel-en-le-Frith) plus sheets SJ96, SJ97, SK04, SK14, SK05, SK15, SK25, SK06, SK16, SK26, SK36, SK07, SK17, SK27, SK37, SE00, SE10, SE20, SE01 to cover the rest of the National Park.

Guidebook

MONKHOUSE, PATRICK, editor, *Peak District National Park*, HMSO, 1971.

Footpath Guides

HAWORTH, JAMES, *Walking in Derbyshire: A Detailed Route Guide for Rambling in the Peak District National Park and Adjacent Countryside*, 5th edn, Derbyshire Countryside Ltd, 1974.

HAWORTH, JAMES, *Walks in the Derbyshire Dales: 30 Footpath Routes – A Handy Guide to Rambling in Derbyshire*, Derbyshire Countryside Ltd, 1973.

MERRILL, JOHN, *Peak District Walks*, 3rd edn, Dalesman, 1976.

POUCHER, W. A., *The Peak and the Pennines from Dovedale to Hadrian's Wall: A Pictorial Guide to Walking in the Region and to the Safe Ascent of its Hills and Moors*, Constable, 1973.

THOMPSON, CLIFFORD, *Peak District Walks for Motorists: Thirty Walks*, Gerrard Publications, 1973.

Pembrokeshire Coast

The Pembrokeshire Coast National Park is the smallest of the parks, covering an area of 225 square miles. It is quite different in character from the other parks in that it has only a small tract of moorland in the Prescelly Hills, but its chief glory is its large area of magnificent, unspoiled coastal scenery. There are many prehistoric remains in the park and a surprisingly large number of medieval castles.

Information Centres
Broad Haven – Pembrokeshire Countryside Unit, Car Park (Tel. 412)
Fishguard – Town Hall (Tel. 3484)
Haverfordwest – County Museum, Haverfordwest Castle (Tel. 3708)
Kilgetty – Kingsmoor Common (Tel. Saundersfoot 813672)
Milford Haven – Town Hall (Tel. 4567)
Pembroke – Drill Hall, Main Street (Tel. 2143)
St David's – City Hall (Tel. 392)
Tenby – The Norton (Tel. 3510)

Rescue Posts
None

Maps
1:50000 sheets 145, 157, 158
1:25000 sheets SR89, SR99, SM70, SM80, SM90, SM71, SM81, SM91, SM62, SM72, SM82, SM73, SM83, SM93, SM84, SM94, SS09, SS19, SN00, SN10, SN01, SN02, SN12, SN03, SN13, SN04, SN14

Guidebook
MILES, DILLWYN, editor, *Pembrokeshire Coast National Park*, HMSO, 1973.

Footpath Guides
The only guides are to the Pembrokeshire Coast Path (see p. 177).

Snowdonia

The Snowdonia National Park is the second largest of the parks, covering an area of 845 square miles. It covers the coastline from Aberdovey to just north of Harlech and is then bounded by the towns of Conway, Bala and Machynlleth. Snowdon (3,560 ft) is the highest mountain in England and Wales and the Snowdon range contains some of the wildest country in Britain, with numerous lakes to enhance

the beauty of the mountains. Over the years, much slate has
been quarried and this park is under constant threat from
industry thirsting to create more reservoirs and hungry to
exploit its minerals.

Information Centres
Aberdyfi – The Wharf (Tel.321)
Bala – Old British School, High Street (Tel. 367)
Blaenau Ffestiniog – Caerblaidd Offices, Queen's Bridge (Tel.
360)
Conway – Old Gas Showrooms (Tel. 2248)
Dolgellau – Bridge End (Tel. 422888)

RESCUE TEAMS

Name	Hon. Secretary
Ogwen Valley MR Organization	The Secretary, Ogwen Cottage, Outdoor Pursuits Centre, Bethesda, Caernarvonshire
Plas-y-Brenin MRT	The Director, National Mountaineering Centre, Plas-y-Brenin, Capel Curig, Caernarvonshire
Moelwyn MRT	P/S Wm Williams, c/o Police Station, Blaenau Ffestiniog
Llanberis MRT	S. H. Rees, 8 Pant y Waen, Waenfawr, Caernarvonshire
Outward Bound	The Warden, Major G. Richards, Outward Bound, Aberdovey, Merioneth
Joint Services Mountain Training Centre, Morfa Camp, Tywyn	The Commandant, Brigadier J. A. Marchant (retd), JSMTC, Tywyn, Merioneth
The Rhinog MRT	G. Ross, Post Office, Llanbedr, Merioneth, LL45 2HH
North Wales Cave Rescue Organization	Alan H. Hawkins, Grove Cottage, Grove Road, Great Mollington, Chester
Search and Rescue Dog Association (Wales)	Chris Wharmby, Tyn r Ardd, Nant Bwleh yr Haearn, Trefriw, Gwynedd
RAF Valley MRT	Officer in Charge, MRT, RAF Valley, Anglesey.

MANNED POSTS

Location	Grid Reference	Telephone
Youth Hostel, Idwal Cottage Bethesda,	SH 649 603	Bethesda 225
Ogwen Cottage Mountain School Bethesda	SH 650 603	Bethesda 214 and 581
Capel Curig, Plas-y-Brenin	SH 716 578	Capel Curig 214 and 230
Pen-y-Gwryd Hotel	SH 660 558	Llanberis 211 and 368
National Park Wardens Centre, Nant Peris, Llanberis	SH 606 584	Llanberis 399
Police Station, Pen-y-Groes	SH 472 533	
Aberglaslyn Hall Mountain Centre, Beddgelert	SH 594 460	Beddgelert 233
Police Station, Blaenau Ffestiniog	SH 704 458	Ffestiniog 252
Police Station, Llandudno	SH 781 823	Llandudno 78241
Aberdovey Outward Bound	SN 627 964	Aberdovey 464
Outdoor Activities Centre, Plas-yr-Antur, Fairborne	SH 614 130	Fairborne 282
Police Station, Barmouth		

OTHER POSTS

Snowdon Summit Hotel		(closed in winter)
Foel Grach	SH 689 659	Refuge shelter only. No equipment
ILEA Centre, Tyn y Berth, Corris	SH 738 092	Corris 678

For rescue go to the rescue post or telephone, whichever is quicker. Dial 999, ask for the police. The position of a post is sometimes changed. Verify locally.

Maps

1:126720 (½ in. to the mile) Tourist map of Snowdonia

1:50000 sheets 115, 116, 124, 125, 135

1:25000 sheets SN59, SN69, SN79, SH50, SH60, SH70, SH80,
SH51, SH61, SH71, SH81, SH91, SH52, SH62, SH72, SH82,
SH92, SH53, SH63, SH73, SH83, SH93, SH44, SH54, SH64,
SH74, SH84, SH94, SH45, SH55, SH65, SH75, SH85, SH66,
SH76, SH86, SH67, SH77, SJ03

Guidebook

EDWARDS, G. RHYS, *Snowdonia National Park*, HMSO.

Footpath Guides

HELLIWELL, ROLAND, *The Idwal Log: Rambles and Scrambles in
the Ogwen District*, 3rd edn, Merseyside Youth Hostels Ltd, 40
Hamilton Square, Birkenhead, 1974.

JONES, I. W., *Betws-y-Coed and the Conway Valley*, John Jones Ltd,
41 Lochaber Street, Cardiff, 1974.

PERRY, S. M., *Welsh Northern Footpaths*, James Pike Ltd, St Ives,
Cornwall, 1975.

POUCHER, W. A., *The Welsh Peaks: A Pictorial Guide to Walking in
This Region and to the Safe Ascent of its Principal Mountain Groups*,
5th edn, Constable, 1973.

ROWLAND, E. G., *The Ascent of Snowdon: The Six Classic Routes up
Snowdon*, 5th edn, Cicerone Press, 16 Briarfield Road, Worsley,
Manchester, 1973.

STYLES, SHOWELL, *Snowdon Range*, West Col Productions, 1973.

STYLES, SHOWELL, *Walking Snowdonia*, John Jones Ltd, 41 Lochaber Street, Cardiff.

WILLIAMS, C., and LIGHT, H., *The Snowdon Log: Rambles and
Scrambles in the Snowdon District*, 3rd edn, Merseyside Youth
Hostels Ltd, 40 Hamilton Square, Birkenhead, 1971.

Yorkshire Dales

The Yorkshire Dales National Park is the third largest park
and covers an area of 680 square miles bounded by the towns
of Skipton, Settle, Sedburgh and Richmond. The Dales
themselves with their enchanting villages are long, narrow
valleys which cut into the Pennines. This is wonderful
country for the walker and, except for one or two places such

as Malham and Kettlewell, relatively uncrowded. One of
the features of the Dales is the scars where the rocks have
slipped leaving the limestone as a huge cliff as at Malham
Cove and Gordale Scar.

Information Centres

Aysgarth Falls – Leyburn (Tel. Aysgarth 424)
Clapham (via Lancaster) – Reading Room (Tel. 419)
Hawes (caravan) – Station Yard – Tuesdays and weekends only
Malham – Car park (Tel.Airton 363)
Settle – Town Hall (Tel. 3617)

RESCUE TEAMS

Name	*Hon. Secretary*
Swaledale Fell Rescue Organization	Mrs M. Salmon, Burnside, Reeth, Richmond, North Yorks
Upper Wharfedale Fell Rescue Association	C. Baker, Clifford House, Intake Lane, Grassington, Skipton, North Yorks
RAF Leeming MRT	Officer in Charge, MRT, RAF Leeming, Northallerton, Yorks

SEARCH DOGS

Search and Rescue Dog Association (England)	B. Veevers, Fence Gate Restaurant, Fence in Pendle, Burnley, Lancs K. G. Saxby, County Police Station, Mickleton, Barnard Castle, Co. Durham, DL12 0LL

MANNED POSTS

Location	*Grid Reference*	*Telephone*
Police Station, Settle	SD 820 635	Settle 2542
National Park Information Centre, Malham	SD 900 626	Airton 363
Police Station, Grassington	SD 995 638	Grassington 752222

Location	Grid Reference	Telephone
Burnside, Reeth	SE 042 992	Reeth 298
National Park Information Centre, Aysgarth Falls, Wensleydale	SE 011 888	Aysgarth 424

For rescue go to the rescue post or telephone, whichever is quicker. Dial 999, ask for the police. The position of a post is sometimes changed. Verify locally.

Maps
1 : 50000 sheets 91, 92, 97, 98, 99, 103, 104
1 : 25000 The Three Peaks Outdoor Leisure map. Malham and Upper Wharfedale Outdoor Leisure map

Guidebook
SIMMONS, I. G., *Yorkshire Dales National Park*, HMSO, 1971.

Footpath Guides
POUCHER, W. A., *The Peak and the Pennines from Dovedale to Hadrian's Wall: A Pictorial Guide to Walking in the Region and to the Safe Ascent of its Hills and Moors*, Constable, 1973.

RAMBLERS' ASSOCIATION, *Further Dales Walks for Motorists: Thirty Circular Walks*, Gerrard Publications, 1970.

RAMBLERS' ASSOCIATION, *Rambles in the Dales: Twenty Selected Walks in the Yorkshire Dales*, Gerrard Publications, 1968.

RAMBLERS' ASSOCIATION, *Walking in Airedale*, Dalesman, 1972.

RAMBLERS' ASSOCIATION, *Walking in the Northern Dales*, Dalesman, 1976.

SPEAKMAN, COLIN, *Walking in the Craven Dales*, 2nd edn, Dalesman, 1973.

WAINWRIGHT, ALFRED W., *Walks in Limestone Country*, Westmorland Gazette, 1970.

WAINWRIGHT, ALFRED W., *Walks on the Howgill Fells*, Westmorland Gazette, 1972.

WHITE, GEOFFREY, *Walks in Wensleydale*, Dalesman, 1976.

AREAS OF
OUTSTANDING
NATURAL BEAUTY

Areas of Outstanding Natural Beauty (known as AONBs) are areas where the landscape is of such a quality that the Countryside Commission and the local authorities have decided to submit formally to the Secretary of State for the Environment a request that the region be declared an Area of Outstanding Natural Beauty.

Once an AONB has been designated the local authority pays particular attention to planning development so that the unique character of the area can be preserved. The local authority remains responsible for AONBs, but they often set up advisory bodies containing representatives from amenity groups which can make recommendations on all matters concerning the area. Not all AONBs make special facilities available for walkers and it does not necessarily follow that paths will be particularly well marked. Nevertheless, their scenic quality alone makes them attractive to walkers and they offer much easier walking than the more rugged parts of National Parks.

There are now thirty-two AONBs and, whereas the number of National Parks in England and Wales is unlikely to be increased, the process for designating AONBs is much simpler and the number is gradually increasing. It is quite cheering to look at a map of England and Wales showing National Parks and AONBs and note just how much of our countryside is now under some form of protection.

Unfortunately, the boundaries of AONBs are not shown on Ordnance Survey maps, but their approximate area is indicated on the map on pp. 124–5. I have given a brief description of each AONB below, together with the sheet numbers of the relevant Ordnance Survey maps and details of any footpath guides I have been able to trace. I have also given the name of the Regional Tourist Board responsible for the area, as many of them have leaflets giving details of walks which they will be pleased to supply on request. The address of each Regional Tourist Board is given on pp. 248–9. The Wales Tourist Board has no regional offices and inquiries should be made to the address given on p. 257. In some cases the local authority produces information about walks and it may be worthwhile to write to the County Planning Officer, whose address can be obtained from *The Municipal Yearbook* which can be consulted in most public libraries.

Anglesey

An area of 84 square miles covering nearly all of this island off the coast of North Wales, forming part of the county of Gwynedd. The scenery may be described as a low plateau with a few isolated hills rising to just over 700 ft and containing a number of shallow valleys. The coastline is particularly attractive, with a series of crescent-shaped bays and rocky headlines. There are fine views across to the mountains of Snowdonia. The island has numerous prehistoric remains.

Maps
1:50000 sheet 114
1:25000 sheets SH27, SH28, SH29, SH36, SH37, SH38, SH39, SH46, SH48, SH49, SH56, SH57, SH58, SH67, SH68

Footpath Guides
None.

Wales Tourist Board

Arnside and Silverdale

Situated on the north-east shore of Morecambe Bay on the southern tip of the Lake District National Park in the counties of Cumbria and Lancashire. This is limestone country with hills up to 500 ft high giving splendid views over Morecambe Bay and to the mountains of the Lake District. The particular charm of this AONB lies in its miniature landscape.

Maps
1 : 50000 sheet 97
1 : 25000 sheets SD47 and SD48

Footpath Guides
None.

North West Regional Tourist Board

Cannock Chase

An area of 26 square miles near Stafford which is one of the traditional lungs of the Black Country. The landscape is made up of bracken-clad heathland and woods broken up by attractive valleys. There are access agreements for the wilder parts of the Chase and some of it is now free from traffic and specially reserved for walkers and riders. It is not really suitable for a walking holiday as the area is too con-fined.

Maps
1 : 50000 sheet 127
1 : 25000 sheets SJ91, SJ92, SK01, SK02

Footpath Guides
A number of outdoor trails leaflets are available from the County Planning Officer, as is the Cannock Chase map showing footpaths.

Heart of England Regional Tourist Board

Chichester Harbour

29 square miles of harbour and estuary around Chichester and Emsworth in West Sussex and Hampshire. This is pre-eminently a sailing centre and, although the salt marshes are very attractive, it is not primarily an area for a walking holiday.

Maps

1:50000 sheet 197

1:25000 sheets SU30, SU40, SU70, SH80, SZ29, SZ39, SZ49, SZ79, SZ89

Footpath Guide

RAMMELL, J.C., and RUSH L.H.H., *A Rambler's Atlas of Western Sussex*, Vol. 2, Collin and French Ltd, 1976.

SHIPPAM, CHARLES, *Twenty Walks West of Arun*, Phillimore, 1973.

South East Regional Tourist Board

The Chilterns

An area of chalk hills stretching in a broad band from Goring-on-Thames to Luton in the counties of Oxfordshire, Buckinghamshire, Hertfordshire and Bedfordshire. Very popular with Londoners as it is so easy to reach by train or car. It contains some excellent walking country with well-defined paths. The area is famous for its attractive and stately beech woods, lovely villages and extensive views over the flat plains to the north.

Maps

1:50000 sheets 165, 166, 175

1:25000 sheets TL01, TL02, TL03, TL12, TL13, SP91, SP92, SP90, TL00, TQ09, SP81, SP70, SP80, SU79, SU89, SU99, SU78, SU88, TQ09, SU67, SU68, SU69, SU70, SU79

Footpath Guides

BURDEN, VERA, *Round Walks West of London*, Spurbooks, 1974.

CHILTERN SOCIETY, *Walks in the Thames-side Chilterns*, Spurbooks, 1973.

CULL, ELIZABETH, *Walks along the Ridgeway*, Spurbooks, 1975.

DAWES, FRANK, *Walks in Hertfordshire*, Spurbooks, 1975.

PIGRAM, RONALD, *Discovering Walks in the Chilterns*, Shire Publications, 1972.

Thames and Chilterns Regional Tourist Board

Cornwall

Cornwall is a county of contrasts. It contains some of the finest coastal scenery in England and some of the interior is very attractive, especially Bodmin Moor. Unfortunately, much of Cornwall outside the designated area is dull and spoiled by ribbon development and clay workings.

Maps
1:50000 sheets 190, 200, 201, 203, 204
1:25000 sheets SW32, SW33, SW42, SW43, SW52, SW53, SW54, SW61, SW62, SW64, SW71, SW72, SW73, SW74, SW75, SW83, SW84, SW86, SW87, SW93, SW94, SW97, SX04, SX05, SX07, SX08, SX15, SX16, SX17, SX18, SX19, SX25, SX26, SX27, SX28, SX29, SX44, SX45, SS20, SS21

Footpath Guides
See guides to the South-West Peninsula Path (p. 188).

West Country Regional Tourist Board

The Cotswolds

Contained by the towns of Bath, Cheltenham and Cirencester, the 582 square miles contain hills of limestone and sandstone from which the buildings of the exceptionally beautiful villages have been constructed. Excellent walking country in the counties of Gloucester, Hereford and Worcester, Oxfordshire, Avon and Wiltshire.

Maps
1:50000 sheets 150, 151, 163, 164, 172, 173
1:25000 sheets SO70, SO80, SO81, SO90, SO91, SO92, SO93, SO94, SP00, SP01, SP02, SP03, SP10, SP11, SP12, SP13, SP14, SP20, SP21, SP22, SP23, ST76, ST77, ST78, ST79, ST87, ST88, ST89, ST98, ST99

Footpath Guides
DRINKWATER, P., and HARGREAVES, H., *Cotswold Rambles*, Thornhill Press, 1975.
HODGES, R., *Walking in the Cotswolds*, Spurbooks, 1976.

KERSHAW, RONALD, and ROBSON, BRIAN, *Discovering Walks in the Cotswolds*, Shire Publications, 1974.

PRICE, PETER A., *Cotswold Walks for Motorists*, Gerrard Publications, 1975.

WISE, PATRICK, *Cotswold Walkabout No. 1*, 1971; *No. 2*, 1972; *No. 3*, 1973; *No. 4*, 1974, The Welsh Shop, Burford, Oxon.

Heart of England Regional Tourist Board

Dedham Vale

22 square miles of the Constable country between Manningtree in Essex and Wayland in Suffolk. It is full of picturesque villages and is a 'typically English' pastoral landscape. Too small for a walking holiday.

Maps
1:50000 sheets 155, 168, 169
1:25000 sheets TM03, TM13, TL93

Footpath Guides
None.

East Anglia Regional Tourist Board

Dorset

Over one-third of Dorset, including nearly the whole of the coastline amounting to 400 square miles, was designated in 1957. Apart from the splendid coastal and downland scenery, the area contains extensive prehistoric remains including Maiden Castle.

Maps
1:50000 sheets 193, 194, 195
1:25000 sheets SY39, SY49, SY59, SY69, SY79, SY58, SY68, SY78, SY88, SY98, SY97, SY67, SZ07, SZ08

Footpath Guides
OSBORNE, G. H., *Walks in Dorset*, Spurbooks, 1974.

West Country Regional Tourist Board

East Devon

Bordering on the western edge of the Dorset AONB, the East Devon AONB covers 103 square miles. It runs westward as far as Exmouth and inland as far as Honiton although small areas around Seaton, Beer and Sidmouth are excluded. The area contains some fine coastal scenery including some of the magnificent red cliffs so typical of Devon. Inland are found charming villages and lovely rolling farmland.

Maps
1:50000 sheets 192, 193
1:25000 sheets ST10, ST11, SY08, SY09, SY18, SY19, SY28, SY29, SY39

Footpath Guides
None.

West Country Regional Tourist Board

East Hampshire

A triangular area of 161 square miles of rolling farmland on the Hampshire/Sussex borders between Winchester and Petersfield. Apart from the fine downland scenery, there is in the area the birthplace of cricket and Butser Hill farm – an iron-age farm which is being run experimentally just as the original farmers tilled the ground.

Maps
1:50000 sheets 197, 185, 196, 186
1:25000 sheets SU51, SU61, SU71, SU42, SU52, SU62, SU72, SU53, SU63, SU73, SU83

Footpath Guides
HAGGARD, DENIS, *Rambles in Hampshire and Sussex on Foot and by Car*, Stroudbridge Cottage, Petersfield, Hants, 1971.
HAGGARD, DENIS, *More Rambles in Hampshire and Sussex on Foot and by Car*, Stroudbridge Cottage, Petersfield, Hants, 1972.
TEVIOT, C. J. K. (Lord Teviot), *Walks along the South Downs Way*, Spurbooks, 1973.

South East Regional Tourist Board

Forest of Bowland

Covering an area of 310 square miles of mostly open moorland between Carnforth, Settle and Clitheroe in the counties
of North Yorkshire and Lancashire, this AONB is really
part of the Pennines but is separated from the main valley
of the Lune. Pendle Hill, 1,831 ft high, is famous because
George Fox, the Quaker, climbed it in 1652 and wrote about
it in his journal. It is perhaps even better known for its association with the Pendle witches, who were tried and executed
in 1612.

Maps
1:50000 sheets 97, 98, 103
1:25000 sheets SD53, SD54, SD55, SD56, SD57, SD63, SD64,
SD65, SD66, SD73, SD74, SD75, SD76, SD83, SD84, SD85,
SD86

Footpath Guides
BANKS, GEOFFREY, *Pendleside and Brontë Country Walks*, Gerrard
   Publications, 1975.
LANCASHIRE COUNTY COUNCIL, *Access Areas in the Forest of
   Bowland* (leaflet), from Estates Office, Winkleigh House, Wink-
   leigh Square, Preston.

North West Regional Tourist Board

The Gower

The very first AONB designated in 1956, the Gower is an
area of 73 square miles on a peninsula to the west of
Swansea in the county of West Glamorgan. It contains fine
beaches, coves and sand dunes and has no towns of any size.

Maps
1:50000 sheet 159
1:25000 sheets SS39, SS49, SS59, SS69, SS38, SS48, SS58,
SS68

Footpath Guide
JONES, ROGER, *Thirty Walks in Gower*, Uplands Bookshop Ltd,
   Uplands, Swansea.

Wales Tourist Board

Isle of Wight

73 square miles – approaching two-thirds of the island –
have been designated an AONB, including some of the
finest beaches. The scenery of the interior is rolling downland with charming villages nestling in the valleys. This is
excellent walking country.

Maps
1:50000 sheet 196
1:25000 sheets SZ38, SZ48, SZ58, SZ68, SZ47, SZ57, SZ49,
SZ59

Footpath Guides
HUTCHINGS, RICHARD J., *Fifty Short Walks in the Isle of Wight*,
    Saunders, 1973.
A number of well-produced leaflets are available from the County
Planning Officer.

South East Regional Tourist Board

Kent Downs

Covering an area of 326 square miles and running from
Orpington to Dover, the Kent Downs AONB includes
classic chalk downland scenery which makes for excellent
walking country very popular with Londoners.

Maps
1:50000 sheets 187, 188, 178, 179, 199
1:25000 sheets TQ67, TQ46, TQ56, TQ66, TQ76, TQ86,
TQ45, TQ65, TQ75, TQ85, TQ95, TR05, TR15, TR25,
TQ44, TQ54, TQ94, TR04, TR14, TR24, TR34, TR03,
TR13, TR23, TR33

Footpath Guides
BAGLEY, WILLIAM A., *London Countryside Walks for Motorists, South
    East*, Gerrard Publications, 1976.
CARLEY, JIM, editor, *Rambles in West Kent*, The Ramblers' Asso-
    ciation, 1975.
DAVIS, CYRIL, and GRAY, ANDREW, *Walks on the North Downs.
    Hollingbourne to the Medway*, Swale Footpaths Group, Scillonia,
    Lewson Street, Teynham, Sittingbourne, Kent, 1974.

DOUGALL, DONALD, *Donald Dougall's TV Walkabout*, Midas Books, 1974.

GRAY, ANDREW, *Rambles in the East Kent Downs*, The Ramblers' Association, 1975.

MORECROFT, VICTOR W., *Rambling through Kent*, Kentish Times, 1973.

SMITH, ALAN, editor, *Walks on the North Downs – Doddington and Lenham*. Swale Footpaths Group, Scillonia, Lewson Street, Teynham, Sittingbourne, Kent, 1974.

SPAYNE, JANET, and ICRYNSKI, AUDREY, *Walks in the Hills of Kent*, Spurbooks, 1976.

WALTON, MARJORIE, *Fifteen Walks around Folkestone*, McNerlin Hughes Associates, 91 Sandgate Road, Folkestone, 1973.

South East Regional Tourist Board

Lincolnshire Wolds

The Lincolnshire Wolds are a series of chalk hills rising to some 500 ft which run from the north-east corner of the county, parallel to the sea, but about 10 miles inland. Because so much of the surrounding countryside is flat, they offer extensive views over the coast and fen. Potentially very good walking country and well worth exploring.

Maps
1:50000 sheets 121, 122, 113
1:25000 sheets TA10, TA20, TF09, TF19, TF29, TF39, TF18, TF28, TF38, TF27, TF37, TF47, TF36, TF46

Footpath Guides
None.

East Midlands Regional Tourist Board

Lleyn

Lleyn is a peninsula in Gwynedd running westwards into the Irish Sea and containing the towns of Pwllheli, Abersoch, Aberderon and Nevin. Most of the beautiful coastline is included in the 60 square miles of the designated area. This is an exceptionally beautiful and remote area of the country. There are narrow lanes, running through gorse, bracken and rough pasture, white cottages and hills that rise to 1,800 ft giving extensive views across the rocky headlands and tiny harbours and bays of the coast. There is as yet no Definitive Map for this part of Gwynedd so rights of way do not appear on the Ordnance Survey Maps.

Maps
1:50000 sheet 123
1:25000 sheets SH12, SH13, SH22, SH23, SH24, SH32, SH33, SH34, SH44, SH45

Footpath Guides
STYLES, SHOWELL, *Exploring Gwynedd from Porthmadog*, John Jones Ltd, 41 Lochaber Street, Cardiff, 1974.

Wales Tourist Board

Malvern Hills

Lying between Great Malvern and Ledbury, the Malvern Hills AONB covers some 40 square miles of the counties of Gloucestershire, Herefordshire and Worcestershire. There are a number of summits over 1,000 ft high with magnificent views over the lowlands. There are many excellent footpaths and this is fine walking country.

Maps
1:50000 sheets 149, 150
1:25000 sheets SO73, SO74, SO75

Footpath Guide
BAKER, DONNA, *Tracking through Mercia*, Express Logic Ltd, Foley Estate, Hereford, 1975.

Heart of England Regional Tourist Board

Mendip Hills

Stretching from Weston-super-Mare to the cathedral city of Wells in the counties of Avon and Somerset, the Mendip has short turf, limestone walls and typical mountain limestone scenery. There are a number of hills over 1,000 ft high giving extensive views over the Bristol Channel. Wookey Hole and Cheddar Gorge form part of a large cave system for which the area is famous. There are numerous drovers' roads suitable for walking.

Maps
1:50000 sheet 182
1:25000 sheets ST 13, ST 14, ST 22, ST 23, ST 35, ST 45, ST 55, ST 54, ST 56, ST 44

Footpath Guides
None.

West Country Regional Tourist Board

Norfolk Coast

This AONB runs round the Norfolk coast from Kings Lynn to Mundesley and covers 174 square miles of beaches, mud flats and salt marsh. Not particularly good walking country but it appeals greatly to those who love the peculiar atmosphere of flat coastal scenery.

Maps
1:50000 sheets 131, 132, 133, 134
1:25000 sheets TF 53, TF 52, TF 62, TF 63, TF 73, TF 64, TF 74, TF 84, TF 83, TF 94, TF 93, TG 04, TG 03, TG 14, TG 13, TG 24, TG 23, TG 33, TG 42

Footpath Guides
LE SURF, JEANNE, *Rambles in Norfolk*, 6 Attihill Road, Norwich, 1973.
LE SURF, JEANNE, *Thirty More Norfolk Walks*, 6 Attihill Road, Norwich, 1970.

East Anglia Regional Tourist Board

North Devon

The whole of the north Devon coast from the boundary with Cornwall to the Exmoor National Park is included in this 66 square miles of rugged coastline, high cliffs and beautiful seascapes. Contains much beautiful scenery and charming old villages with thatched cottages.

Maps
1:50000 sheets 180, 190
1:25000 sheets SS21, SS22, SS32, SS42, SS43, SS44, SS54, SS64

Footpath Guide
BEER, TREVOR, *Devon's Northern Footpaths*, J. Pike, 1975.

West Country Regional Tourist Board

Northumberland Coast

The Northumberland Coast contains some marvellous scenery in its 50 square miles stretching from Berwick-on-Tweed southwards to Amble. The cold, exposed beaches discourage conventional holidaymakers so it is quite unspoiled. There are magnificent castles, charming fishing villages and Holy Island and the Farne Islands to explore.

Maps
1:50000 sheets 75, 81
1:25000 sheets NU04, NU05, NU13, NU14, NU20, NU21, NU22, NU23

Footpath Guides
None.

Northumbria Regional Tourist Board

North Wessex Downs

The largest AONB yet designated covers 671 square miles in Hampshire, Wiltshire, Oxfordshire and Berkshire, bordered by the towns of Reading, Newbury, Andover, Devizes and Swindon. This area contains the largest and least-spoiled tract of chalk downland in southern England. There are several hills over 900 ft high and the area includes some of the most important prehistoric sites in the country. Very good walking country.

Maps
1:50000 sheets 185, 174, 184, 173
1:25000 sheets SU54, SU55, SU45, SU34, SU36, SU35, SU44, SU46, ST96, SU18, SU28, SU07, SU17, SU27, SU37, SU06, SU16, SU26, SU05, SU15, SU25, SU35, SU38, SU48, SU58, SU59, SU47, SU57, SU67, SU56, SU66

Footpath Guides
CHAPMAN, ROY, *Walks Around the Downs*, Countryside Books, 4 Turnets Drive, Thatcham, Berks, 1976.
CULL, ELIZABETH, *Walks along the Ridgeway*, Spurbooks, 1976.
RAMBLERS' ASSOCIATION, *Rambling for Pleasure around Maidenhead*, Ramblers' Association, East Berkshire Group, 1975.
RAMBLERS' ASSOCIATION, *Nine Downland Walks South of Swindon*, Ramblers' Association, Wiltshire Area, 1975.

Quantock Hills

The Quantocks are a range of hills in Somerset which run from just north of Taunton to Watchet on the coast. 38 square miles have now been designated and the area includes wooded combes and valleys, bracken-clad hills and picturesque villages.

Maps
1:50000 sheets 181, 182, 183
1:25000 sheets ST35, ST44, ST45, ST54, ST55

Footpath Guides
None.

West Country Regional Tourist Board

Shropshire Hills

An irregularly shaped AONB to the south of Shrewsbury including the towns of Wellington, Church Stretton and Craven Arms. In the 300 square miles of the designated area will be found some fine walking in the hills, which rise in places to nearly 1,800 ft giving some splendid views.

Maps
1:50000 sheet 126
1:25000 sheets SO38, SO39, SO48, SO49

Footpath Guide
SMART, ROBERT, *Church Stretton Rambles*, 2nd edn, Brackendale, Longhills Road, Church Stretton, Salop, 1973.

Heart of England Regional Tourist Board

Solway Coast

The Solway Coast AONB stretches from the Scottish border to Maryport in Cumbria and covers an area of 41 square miles overlooking the Solway Firth to Scotland. Although the area is flat, containing fine sandy beaches, the views across to the hills of Scotland are magnificent.

Maps
1:50000 sheet 97
1:25000 sheets SD47, SD48

Footpath Guide
WOOD, MARGARET A., *Read about Walks on the English Solway Coast*, Photo Precision Ltd, 1975.

English Lakes Regional Tourist Board

South Devon

One of the most popular holiday areas in the country, the South Devon AONB runs from Plymouth to Torbay including most of the South Hams and covering 128 square miles. This region is famous for its fine beaches, cliff scenery and the beautiful estuaries and inlets that stretch for miles inland.

Maps
1:50000 sheets 201, 202
1:25000 sheets SX44, SX45, SX54, SX55, SX63, SX64, SX65, SX73, SX74, SX75, SX83, SX84, SX85, SX94, SX95

Footpath Guide
GRAY, MARY, *Devon's Southern Footpaths*, J. Pike, 1975.

West Country Regional Tourist Board

South Hampshire Coast

This, like Chichester Harbour AONB, is a famous sailing centre and covers 30 square miles from just east of Beaulieu to west of Lymington with the northern edge bordered by the New Forest.

Maps
1:50000 sheets 195, 196
1:25000 sheets SU70, SU80

Footpath Guides
None.

South East Regional Tourist Board

Suffolk Coast and Heaths

This area contains 150 square miles of coast from Ipswich and the Orwell estuary almost to Lowestoft. The region is very flat and contains some beautifully wooded estuaries and many creeks which are the haunt of wild fowl.

Maps
1:50000 sheets 156, 169
1:25000 sheets TM13, TM14, TM23, TM24, TM25, TM33, TM34, TM35, TM44, TM45, TM46, TM47, TM48, TM57, TM58

Footpath Guides
None.

East Anglia Regional Tourist Board

Surrey Hills

Another popular walking area for Londoners, the Surrey Hills AONB contains 160 square miles of chalk downland

and greensand and stretches from Farnham and Haslemere eastwards to the Kent boundary. The greensand hills, which include Leith Hill at 965 ft (the highest point in south-east England), run to the south of the chalk downs and offer contrasting vegetation of bracken and silver birches and magnificent views across the weald to the South Downs and even to the sea from one or two places.

Maps
1:50000 sheets 186, 187
1:25000 sheets SU83, SU84, SU93, SU94, TQ03, TQ04, TQ05, TQ14, TQ15, TQ25, TQ35, TQ45

Footpath Guides
BAGLEY, WILLIAM, A., *London Countryside Walks for Motorists, South-West*, Gerrard Publications, 1976.
HOLLIS, G., *Surrey Walks*, Surrey Advertiser, 1975.
LONDON TRANSPORT, *Country Walks*, Book 3, London Transport, 1975.
SPAYNE, JANET, and KRYINSKI, AUDREY, *Walks in the Surrey Hills*, Spurbooks, 1975.

South East Regional Tourist Board

The Sussex Downs

A series of great whaleback chalk hills that run from Petersfield in West Sussex to Eastbourne in East Sussex and cover 379 square miles. This is fine walking country with extensive views northwards across the weald and southwards to the coast. Near Eastbourne the downs reach the sea and form cliffs over 500 ft high.

Maps
1:50000 sheets 197, 198, 199
1:25000 sheets SU70, SU71, SU72, SU81, SU82, SU83, SU90, SU91, SU92, SU93, TQ00, TQ01, TQ02, TQ10, TQ11, TQ20, TQ21, TQ30, TQ31, TQ40, TQ41, TQ50, TV59

Footpath Guides
DOUGALL, DONALD, *Donald Dougall's TV Walkabout*, Midas, 1974.

EASTBOURNE RAMBLING CLUB, *On Foot in East Sussex*, 5th edn, Eastbourne Rambling Club, 21 Kinfauns Avenue, Eastbourne, 1975.

HAGGARD, DENIS, *Rambles in Hampshire and Sussex on Foot and by Car*, Stroudbridge Cottage, Petersfield, Hants, 1971.

HAGGARD, DENIS, *More Rambles in Hampshire and Sussex on Foot and by Car*, Stroudbridge Cottage, Petersfield, Hants, 1972.

HAGGARD, DENIS, *In and around Storrington*, Stroudbridge Cottage, Petersfield, Hants, 1973.

RAMMELL, J.C., and RUSH, L.H.H., *A Rambler's Atlas of Western Sussex*, 2 vols., Collin and French Ltd, 1976.

SHIPPAM, CHARLES, *Twenty Walks West of Arun*, Phillimore, 1973.

TEVIOT, C. J. K., *South Sussex Walks*, 2nd edn, BBC.

TEVIOT, C. J. K., *Walks along the South Downs Way*, 2nd edition, Spurbooks, 1976.

South East Regional Tourist Board

The Wye Valley

The 124 square miles of the Wye Valley from Chepstow northwards almost to Hereford contains some superb river scenery including, in the lower half, cliffs and gorges. Above Ross, the river is narrower and runs more quickly. This AONB lies in the counties of Gwent, Hereford and Worcester, and Gloucestershire.

Maps
1:50000 sheets 171, 161, 162, 149, 172
1:25000 Outdoor Leisure map of the Wye Valley

Footpath Guide
JONES, ROGER, *Exploring the Wye Valley and Forest of Dean*, Harvey Barton, 1975.

Heart of England Regional Tourist Board

Bibliography

AUTOMOBILE ASSOCIATION, *No Through Road*, Drive Publications Ltd, 1975.

BUSH, ROGER, *The National Parks of England and Wales together with Areas of Outstanding Natural Beauty and Long Distance Footpaths and Bridleways*, Dent, 1973.
REDFERN, ROGER, *Walking in England*, Hale, 1976.

Although there is not yet a long-distance footpath from
Land's End to the Scottish border, nevertheless there are
continuous footpaths which cover very long stretches of
England and Wales.

The Hobhouse Committee on Footpaths and Access to
the Countryside recommended that continuous rights of way
over some of the country's finest mountain, moorland, downland and coastal scenery be created. The National Parks and
Access to the Countryside Act, 1949 provided the necessary
legislation for creating such long-distance footpaths. These
paths were always intended to be based on some strong
physical or historic feature so they are not merely routes for
getting from one place to another.

The Countryside Commission is responsible for recommending to the Secretary of State for the Environment
routes for long-distance paths. Once the Minister has approved the recommendation, the Countryside Commission
assists local authorities in establishing the exact line of the
path and negotiating with landowners and other interested
parties.

Often considerable sections of long-distance paths were
already rights of way, but some stretches had to be created
by negotiating with the landowners and paying compensation. One of the most difficult tasks was establishing who
owned the land, but only rarely has it been necessary to
establish a right of way by statute, and obviously it is better
to create paths by negotiation rather than applying the law,
to avoid antagonizing landowners unnecessarily.

Long-distance footpaths are waymarked using the Countryside Commission symbol of an acorn. This is a non-directional sign and should be used merely to confirm that the walker has not strayed from the path. Ordnance Survey maps, or a good footpath guide, are necessary to walk these paths accurately. The 1:25000 map should be used for all of them except, perhaps, for the Pennine Way and the Cleveland Way, where the smaller-scale map may suffice, especially if supplemented with one of the guides to these Ways.

Walking one of the long-distance paths is something of an adventure. The walker sees the countryside in a way that no other traveller does and will be surprised at how empty our densely populated country is once the main roads are foresaken. Much pleasure can be had in planning a long-distance walk. Nights spent poring over maps, bus and railway timetables and accommodation directories will give many anticipatory thrills.

The biggest problem is likely to be accommodation. Camping would seem to offer the greatest flexibility, but not all the long-distance paths are suitable for camping because they often lack convenient sites and water. It is advisable to book accommodation well in advance especially during the busier seasons of the year. Blazing sunshine is not essential to enjoy a walking holiday, indeed walking in great heat is usually uncomfortable, so it is worth considering an out-of-season holiday. The countryside is very beautiful in spring and autumn and can be enjoyable in the winter months when the bare beauty of the trees is so attractive. But neither the Pennine Way nor the Cleveland Way should be attempted between November and April except by the hardiest and most experienced walkers.

It is not necessary to complete a long-distance path in consecutive days, although this method is probably the most enjoyable, and gives the greatest sense of achievement. With careful planning, it is often possible to walk a path in a series of weekends or even odd days.

Long-distance paths are for pleasure and recreation, not

record breaking. There is no merit in walking the Pennine Way in fourteen days rather than fifteen. Some people like to walk a long distance each day with only a few stops; others like to dawdle, pausing frequently to observe what is going on around them. The style of walking, whether it be purposeful or lackadaisical, does not matter, except that any companion must be of a similar temperament to oneself. Before attempting any of the long-distance paths, walkers should have a clear idea of their walking abilities and know how much ground they can cover each day. If carrying heavy packs, it is advisable to do some practice walking with a full rucksack to become accustomed to it.

The Cleveland Way

The Cleveland Way starts at Helmsley on the edge of the North York Moors National Park and runs for 100 miles around three sides of the park to finish at Filey on the coast. The scenery varies between moorland and magnificent cliffs along the coast.

The path leaves Helmsley skirting Duncombe Park before crossing the River Rye about half a mile from the ruins of Rievaulx Abbey. It follows wooded valleys to Cold Kirby to reach the steep cliff at Sutton Bank with fine views across the Vale of York to the Pennines. There follows a cliff edge walk above Gormire Lake, along Boltby Scar to Sneck Yat, until the old drove road is picked up at High Paradise. After climbing to some 1,200 ft the path leaves the drove road in Oakdale and reaches Osmotherley.

Just north of Osmotherley, the path joins the line of the Lyke Wake Walk for 12 miles and then crosses Carlton Bank, Cringle Moor, Cold Moor and Hasty Bank. Next comes Urra Moor and Botton Head, which at 1,500 ft is the highest point of the North York Moors. At Blaworth Crossing, the path turns north-north-west to the top of Greenhow Bank, Battesby Bank and on to Kildale.

From Kildale the path climbs Easby Moor to the monument to Captain Cook and then over Great Ayton Moor

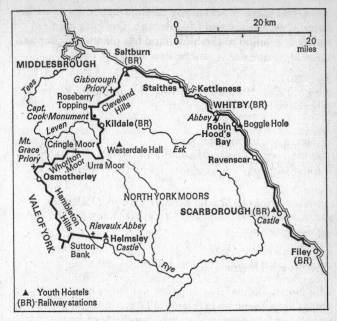

Fig. 28 The Cleveland Way

and on to Highcliff, Guisborough and Skelton and so to the sea at Saltburn.

The rest of the walk is a coastal path over Boulby Cliff, the highest cliff on the English coast, to the charming fishing village of Staithes and on to Runswick, Lythe Bank and Whitby. Past Whitby, the path goes on to the North Cheek of Robin Hood's Bay to finish just short of Filey. The energetic can then start the Wolds Way at Filey and finish at North Ferriby (see p. 190).

This part of England is blessed with a dry climate, but it can be bleak and cold. It is not a difficult walk but considerably harder than the Ridgeway and the North and South Downs, and it is advisable to dress as for fell-walking.

Accommodation is plentiful in parts, especially along the

coast, but there is practically nothing in the 25 miles between Osmotherley and Guisborough. Camping seems to be the ideal solution as the hinterland has plenty of water and there are numerous organized sites along the coast.

Youth Hostels
Boggle Hole, Helmsley, Saltburn, Scarborough, Westerdale, Wheeldale, Whitby.

Maps
1:50000 sheets 101, 94, 93, 99, 100
1:25000 sheets TA08, SE99, NZ90, NZ81, NZ71, NZ62, NZ61, NZ51, NZ60, NZ50, NZ40, SE49, SE48, SE58, SE68

Guides
COWLEY, WILLIAM, *The Cleveland Way*, 3rd edn, Dalesman, 1975.
FALCONER, A., *The Cleveland Way*, HMSO, 1972. (The better guide for walkers)

The North Downs Way

The North Downs Way runs for 141 miles over the chalk downs from Farnham in Surrey to Dover in Kent. There is a popular misconception that the long-distance footpath follows the line of the ancient Pilgrim's Way. It does in one or two places, but the route was chosen for its scenic qualities not for its historical associations.

The path starts very conveniently at Farnham railway station on the Waterloo line, follows the River Wey for a short distance, then climbs to the north of Crooksbury Hill, passes the village of Seale, keeping just south of the summit of the Hog's Back, and continues to Puttenham. It then passes under the A3, the Guildford By-pass, to the River Wey navigation on the southern side of Guildford, where it joins the historic Pilgrim's Way to climb St Martha's Hill with its tiny chapel and over Newlands Corner and Albury Downs to Netley Heath, White Down and Ranmore Common to the A24 at Box Hill.

Box Hill is one of those curious places where vast numbers of people congregate on fine weekends. One edge of the hill

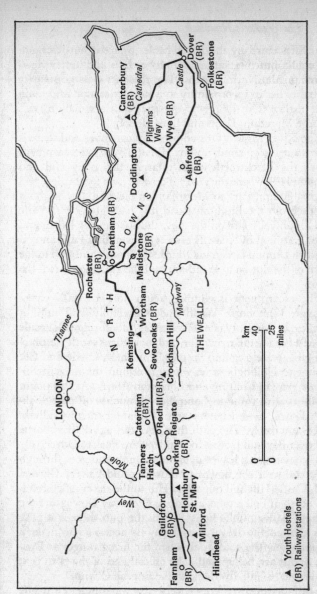

Fig. 29 The North Downs Way

is a cliff formed by the River Mole, where it cuts through the chalk, but there are many higher hills and better viewpoints on the North Downs. The reason for its popularity probably lies in its proximity to a railway station and main road rather than its scenic qualities and association with George Meredith, Keats and Lord Nelson.

The River Mole is crossed by stepping stones and there is then a very steep climb up Box Hill and over the escarpment above the Betchworth chalk quarries to Colley Hill and Reigate Hill, where the A 217 is crossed by a footbridge, and on past Gatton Park to Merstham on the A 23, the Brighton Road. From the Brighton Road, the path goes over White Hill to Gravelly Hill on the A 22, the Eastbourne Road, and on to Tatsfield in Kent. It crosses Chevenning Park and on through Dunton Green to Otford. The path climbs up to the scarp of the downs to Wrotham and the Hastings Road, the A 20.

The escarpment is climbed again and the path passes through Whitehorse Wood and over Holly Hill until it reaches the Medway near Rochester. A footbridge alongside the M 2 crosses the river. The path now turns south via Bluebell Hill to Detling and on past Thurnham Castle and Cat Mount to Hollingbourne, where it rejoins the ancient Pilgrim's Way to Charing and Boughton Aluph. At this point, an alternative route to Canterbury branches off past Soakham Down, Godmersham and Chilham Park to Chilham and Canterbury. The path then goes through Patrixbourne and over Barham Downs to Waldershare Park to Dover.

The main path leaves Boughton Aluph and goes through Wye and over the downs to Stowting and Cherry Garden Hill, Castle Hill and Sugarloaf Hill to the main A 620 road, just north of Folkestone, and on to Creteway Downs and the Valiant Sailor public house. From the pub there is a path over the cliffs to Dover but it may be necessary to make a detour along the coast road when the firing ranges at Lyddon Spout are being used. The official end of the path is at Shakespeare Cliff, overlooking the English Channel.

The North Downs Way is very easy walking and a strong

walker could do it comfortably in one week. Accommodation tends to be sparse but it should not be too difficult to find bed and breakfast establishments or inns in some of the towns along the route. Many of the main roads that cross the Way have bus services to nearby towns. It is not really practicable to camp as there are few suitable sites and no potable water on the downs. This walk is very easy to do in occasional day-trips from London as there are so many railway stations along the route. No special kit or equipment is required. Only the section from Boughton Aluph to Dover has been officially designated so far.

Youth Hostels
Tanner's Hatch, Holmbury St Mary, Crockham Hill, Doddington, Canterbury, Dover.

Maps
1:50000 sheets 178, 179, 186, 187, 188, 189
1:25000 sheets SU84, SU94, TQ04, TQ14, TQ15, TQ25, TQ35, TQ45, TQ55, TQ65, TQ66, TQ76, TQ75, TQ85, TQ95, TQ94, TR04, TR05, TR15, TR25, TR24, TR14, TR13, TR23, TR34

Guides
WRIGHT, CHRISTOPHER JOHN, *A Guide to the Pilgrim's Way and the North Downs Way*, Constable, 1971.

Offa's Dyke Path

Offa's Dyke Path runs for 168 miles from near the Severn Bridge to Prestatyn in North Wales. For most of its route, it follows Offa's Dyke, an earthwork constructed by the King of Mercia in the eighth century to mark the boundary between his lands and those of the Welsh.

From the Severn Bridge, the path goes to Chepstow and then climbs Tutshill to Wintour's Leap – a cliff with a magnificent view. It follows the Wye and the Dyke to Shorn Cliff and the Devil's Pulpit, with fine views of Tintern Abbey, and so on to Monmouth, where the Wye and Monnow are crossed. The path follows a route through pleasant

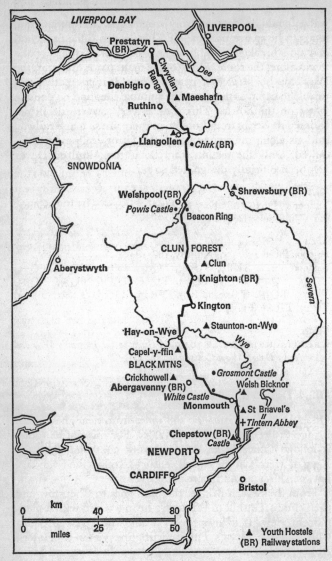

Fig. 30 Offa's Dyke Path

countryside past White Castle before, at Pandy, commencing the long climb up the Black Mountains. A long ridge, rising to 2,000 ft, is crossed before dropping down to Hay-on-Wye.

From Hay, the path goes to Gladestry and Kington, where the Dyke can be clearly seen on Rushock Hill and Herrock Hill. From Knighton, the path follows the Teme and up Panpunton Hill, Llanvair Hill, Spoad Hill and Clun Forest before descending near Montgomery. After crossing the plain actually on the Dyke, the path climbs Long Mountain and Beacon Ring and then reaches the Severn at Buttington. The river is followed for some way but then the path strikes out through Llanymynech to Baker's Hill, past Chirk Castle and crosses the valley of the Dee by the Pontcysyllte aqueduct 120 ft above the valley.

The Vale of Llangollen is now followed to Eglwyseg Mountain, the End of the World and then over the moors to Llandegla where the River Alun is crossed a number of times before reaching the Clwydian Hills, a high ridge walk rising to about 2,000 ft. The path continues through Bodfari and on at last to Prestatyn.

On the whole, this is an easy walk, but the two high sections over the Black Mountains and the Clwydian Hills must be treated with respect, especially in bad weather.

Youth Hostels
Severn Bridge, St Briavels Castle, Capel-y-ffin, Glascwm, Clun Mill, Llangollen, Maeshafn.

Maps
1:50000 sheets 116, 117, 126, 137, 148, 161, 162
1:25000 sheets SJ08, SJ07, SJ16, SJ15, SJ25, SJ24, SJ23, SJ22, SJ21, SJ20, SO29, SO28, SO27, SO26, SO25, SO24, SO23, SO22, SO32, SO31, SO41, SO51, SO50, ST59

Guides
NOBLE, FRANK, *The Shell Book of Offa's Dyke Path*, Queen Anne Press, 1972.
WRIGHT, CHRISTOPHER JOHN, *A Guide to Offa's Dyke Path*, Constable, 1976. (The better guide for walkers)

The Pembrokeshire Coast Path

The Pembrokeshire Coast Path runs for 168 miles from the county border at Poppit Sands about 1½ miles north of St Dogmaels along cliffs, beaches and dunes to the Teifi estuary. As the path follows the extreme edge of the coast, except for one or two places where it has to go inland, it is unnecessary to give the route in detail. The scenery is very

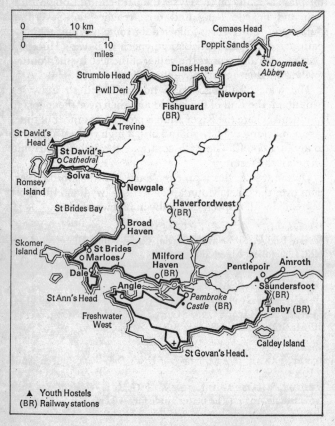

Fig. 31 The Pembrokeshire Coast Path

beautiful and largely unspoiled and it is very easy walking. Accommodation is plentiful but likely to be full at peak holiday times so booking is essential. There are plenty of camp sites and there should be no difficulty in obtaining water. During the summer, there is a special Coast Path bus service which links all the coastal car parks from Dale to Newgale. Walkers should beware of sunburn!

Youth Hostels
Poppit Sands, Pwll Deri, Trevine, St David's Head, Pentlepoir.

Maps
1:50000 sheets 145, 157, 158
1:25000 sheets SN10, SS19, SS09, SR99, SM80, SM90, SM70, SM81, SM82, SM72, SM83, SM93, SN03, SN04, SN14

Guide
BARRETT, JOHN, *The Pembrokeshire Coast Path*, HMSO, 1974.

The Pennine Way

Unquestionably the most famous of the long-distance footpaths, it is also the roughest and toughest and suitable only for experienced fell-walkers. It runs for 270 miles from Edale in Derbyshire to Kirk Yetholm just over the border in Scotland, through some of the wildest scenery in England along the top of the Pennines. One of the fascinations of the Pennine Way is the numerous evidence of old mine workings, drove roads and Roman roads. There are magnificent waterfalls, huge limestone cliffs and, for the naturalist, sub-alpine flora.

From Edale, the path makes a steep ·climb up Grindsbrook to the Kinder plateau, which is 2,000 ft high and a wilderness of quaking peat bogs entirely lacking in proper paths. At Kinder Downfall, which has a fine waterfall after heavy rain (which means in normal conditions!), the path follows the Edge for a short distance and then heads for more peat bogs and the Snake Pass (A57). Beyond the A57 is Bleaklow Hill with many more peat bogs before the path descends to the Crowden reservoir and the A628 road. Now

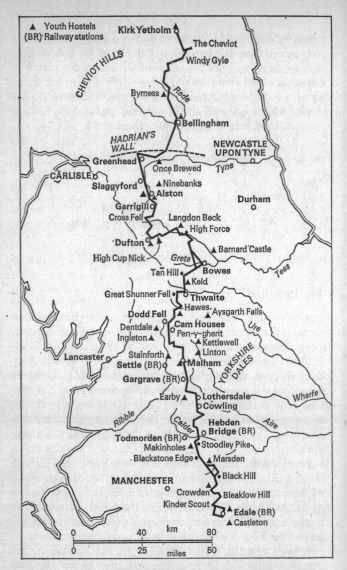

▲ Youth Hostels
(BR) Railway stations

Kirk Yetholm
The Cheviot
Windy Gyle

CHEVIOT HILLS

Byrness ▲
Rede

Bellingham

HADRIAN'S
WALL
Greenhead
Once Brewed
NEWCASTLE
UPON TYNE
CARLISLE
Tyne
Slaggyford
▲ Ninebanks
▲ **Alston**
Durham
Garrigill
Cross Fell
Langdon Beck
▲
High Force
Dufton
▲ Barnard Castle
High Cup Nick
Greta
Tan Hill
Bowes
▲ Keld
Great Shunner Fell ●
Thwaite
Hawes
Aysgarth Falls
Dodd Fell
Dentdale ▲
Cam Houses
Ingleton ▲
Pen-y-ghent
Ure
Kettlewell ▲
Linton
Stainforth
Settle (BR)
Malham
Gargrave (BR)
YORKSHIRE DALES
Earby ▲
Lothersdale
Cowling
Wharfe
LANCASTER
Ribble
Hebden Bridge (BR)
Calder
Aire
Todmorden (BR)
Makinholes ▲
Stoodley Pike
Blackstone Edge ●
▲ Marsden
MANCHESTER
● Black Hill
Crowden
Bleaklow Hill
Kinder Scout
▲ **Edale (BR)**
▲ Castleton

0		40	km	80
0		25	miles	50

Fig. 32 The Pennine Way

follows a long climb to Black Hill, after which the A 62 and M 62 are crossed, the latter near the Holme Moss television mast.

Blackstone Edge follows and then some rather dull walking along a reservoir road to the Calder Valley. This is Brontë country and the Way passes the reputed site of Wuthering Heights on Haworth Moor. Easier walking follows from Lothersdale onwards, especially alongside the beautiful Aire in the Yorkshire Dales National Park. At Malham, one of the most fascinating parts of the route, the path climbs the limestone cliff known as Malham Cove. This was once a waterfall larger than Niagara but now the river goes underground and emerges at the base of the cliff.

After passing Malham Tarn, there is a long slog to the summit of Fountains Fell followed by a descent to the road and another very steep climb up to the marvellous viewpoint of Pen-y-Ghent. From Horton-in-Ribblesdale, there is a fine packhorse trail to Hawes in beautiful Wensleydale. The valley is followed for a short distance passing close to Hardraw Force, a very fine waterfall behind which it is possible to walk. Now begins the long climb up to Great Shunner Fell (2,340 ft) and down again to Thwaite in Swaledale.

From Thwaite there is a long, but easy, ascent over Stonesdale Moor to Tan Hill and the highest pub in England (1,732 ft). The route now divides – one arm going to Bowes and the A 66 and the other, the more direct route, to Blackton reservoir, where the Bowes alternative rejoins the main route before descending to Middleton-in-Teesdale. An easy and beautiful section follows along the river Tees past the famous waterfall of High Force and on to a less well-known, but much more spectacular, waterfall of Cauldron Snout below the Cow Green reservoir. Beyond the reservoir the Way follows the Maize Beck until reaching the natural amphitheatre of High Cup Nick and then descends to Dufton and the Vale of Eden.

After Dufton, the Way climbs up to Knock Fell, Great Dun Fell, Little Dun Fell to Cross Fell, the highest point on the Way (2,930 ft). It is also a magnificent view point, with extensive views to the mountains of the Lake District and to the Scottish border. A steep descent is made to the old corpse road which is followed to Garrigill. The valley of the South Tyne is followed to Alston, Slaggyford and Greenhead.

The Way now follows Hadrian's Wall for several miles, including some of the best-preserved and most spectacular sections, almost to Housesteads, which is one of the most interesting forts on the Wall. Beyond the Wall is a large expanse of forest which makes for dull walking through the quiet and eerie fir trees; then there is a steep climb to Shitlington Crags before dropping down to Bellingham on the River North Tyne. Now follows an easy section along Hareshaw Burn and over Lord's Shaw, Brownrigg Head and through the forest of Redesdale to Byrness.

The last section is one of the toughest of them all. It starts with a very steep climb out of Redesdale to Coquetdale and the Cheviots. For much of the route the border fence helps to define the path through the extensive bogs. There is a short alternative route which goes to the summit of the Cheviot (2,676 ft) for anyone who can summon up sufficient energy. At long last, the path starts to descend until it reaches Kirk Yetholm.

There is a fair amount of bed and breakfast accommodation along the Pennine Way but also some long stretches with no towns or villages. Probably the most satisfactory method is to camp, because there is never any shortage of drinking water, and there are many suitable camp sites on the fells.

Anyone attempting to walk the Pennine Way must be properly equipped and know how to use a map and compass. The weather in the Pennines is notorious for its heavy rainfall, high winds and mists, even in summer.

Youth Hostels
Edale, Crowden, Mankinholes, Earby, Malham, Hawes, Keld, Dufton, Langdon Beck, Alston, Once Brewed, Bellingham, Byrness, Kirk Yetholm.

Maps

1:50000 sheets 74, 80, 86, 91, 92, 98, 103, 109, 110

1:25000 sheets NT82, NT81, NT91, NT92, NT71, NT70, NY79, NY89, NY88, NY87, NY77, NY76, NY66, NY65, NY64, NY74, NY73, NY63, NY72, NY62, NY82, NY83, NY92, NY91, NY90, NY80, SD99, SD89, SD87, SD86, SD96, SD95, SD94, SD93, SD92, SD91, SE01, SE00, SK09, SK08, SK18, SD88

Guides

BINNS, ALAN PENROSE, *Walking the Pennine Way*, 2nd edn, Gerrard Publications, 1972.

MARRIOTT, MICHAEL, *The Shell Book of the Pennine Way*, Queen Anne Press, 1968.

OLDHAM, KENNETH, *The Pennine Way: Britain's Longest Continuous Footpath*, 4th edn, Dalesman, 1972.

STEPHENSON, TOM, *The Pennine Way*, HMSO, 1969.

WAINWRIGHT, ALFRED W., *A Pennine Way Companion*, Westmorland Gazette, 1968. (The best general-purpose guide for walkers)

WRIGHT, C.J., *A Guide to the Pennine Way*, 2nd edn, Constable, 1975.

The Ridgeway

The Ridgeway path runs from Ivinghoe in Buckinghamshire to Overton Hill near Avebury in Wiltshire, a distance of some 85 miles. Its name causes some confusion, as the Great Ridgeway is a prehistoric route which ran from the Wash to Axmouth in Devon. The line of the long-distance path coincides with the Great Ridgeway between Streatley on the Thames and Overton Hill. The first 41 miles uses ancient routes only occasionally. The latter half is all bridleway and thus of interest to riders and cyclists.

The path starts near the village of Ivinghoe at Ivinghoe Beacon, an 800-ft-high summit with extensive views, and then continues, either on the summit or along the scarp, until it descends to cross the Tring gap. It then climbs the escarpment again and takes a high-level route to Wendover, passing through some glorious beechwoods to descend again at Wendover. From Wendover, Coombe Hill is climbed and

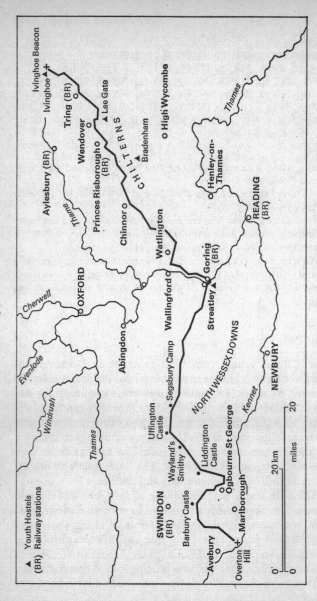

Fig. 33 The Ridgeway Path

▲ Youth Hostels
(BR) Railway stations

there are more beechwoods before the Chequers Estate is crossed by a path. There is more beechwood and downland before the path drops down to Princes Risborough.

There is now a short section on metalled roads before the path takes to the fields and then climbs Lodge Hill before joining the Upper Icknield Way, which at this point is a broad track. This track follows the foot of the scarp for several miles and makes for dull if fast walking passing underneath the M40 and south of Watlington.

Now follows a short stretch of road and then the path heads across Swyncombe Down and through Ewelme Park before turning due west at Nuffield following Grim's Ditch, the ancient boundary, to Mongwell and North Stoke and the River Thames. The path follows the river to Goring and from there takes the road to Streatley.

The Great Ridgeway is now followed across the Berkshire Downs past Segsbury, Whitehorse Hill, Uffington Castle and Wayland's Smithy to Liddington Castle, Barbury Castle and Hackpen Hill before dropping down to West Overton.

The Ridgeway Path is probably the easiest of the long-distance footpaths and requires no special kit except stout shoes. The western end of the path in Wiltshire and Berkshire cannot easily be walked in separate day trips because public transport is so limited, but Londoners can walk the eastern half starting either from Luton or Aylesbury, and catching the bus to Ivinghoe Beacon. There are railway stations at Tring, Wendover and Princes Risborough. Accommodation, too, is limited as this is not really bed and breakfast country, but small inns can be found in some towns. Camping is not recommended as there is no water.

Youth Hostels
Ivinghoe, Lee Gate, Bradenham, Streatley.

Maps
1:50000 sheets 165, 173, 174, 175
1:25000 sheets SU16, SU17, SU27, SU28, SU38, SU48, SU58, SU68, SU69, SU79, SP70, SP80, SP90, SP91

Guides

BURDEN, VERA, *Discovering the Ridgeway*, Shire Publications, 1976.

CULL, ELIZABETH, *Walks along the Ridgeway*, 2nd edn, Spurbooks, 1976.

WESTACOTT, H. D., *A Practical Guide to Walking the Ridgeway Path*, 3rd edn., Footpath Publications, Adstock Cottage, Adstock, Buckingham MK18 2HZ, 1977.

The South Downs Way

The South Downs Way is the only long-distance bridle path yet created so it may be used by riders and cyclists as well as walkers. It runs for some 80 miles from Eastbourne in Sussex to near Petersfield in Hampshire.

The path leaves the outskirts of Eastbourne and then climbs Willingdon Hill, passes through Jevington and crosses Windover Hill to Alfriston. There is an alternative route, for walkers only, starting from Beachy Head and following the cliffs to the Seven Sisters where it turns north to meet the bridleway near Alfriston. From Alfriston, the path climbs the Downs and crosses Firle Beacon to Southease.

The path now turns inland to avoid Brighton, crosses the A27, passes just south of Plumpton and climbs Ditchling Beacon to the A23, south of Pyecombe. There is now another climb to the Devil's Dyke, Edburton Hill and Truleigh Hill before dropping into the Alder Valley near Botolphs. Chanctonbury Ring is the next notable landmark, followed by Highden Hill, Kithurst Hill and Rackham Hill to Amberley station. Next comes Bury Hill, Bignor Hill, Burton Down, Woolavington Down, Graffham Down and so to the A286 south of Cocking. The path now crosses Linch Down, Philliswood Down and Beacon Hill to the B2141 and B2146 near South Harting.

This is easy walking on the downland turf. Although there are some stiff climbs, no special kit or equipment is required. There is an excellent rail network which crosses the path at several points and the Southdown bus services are very good. It is quite practicable, with some planning, to walk this path

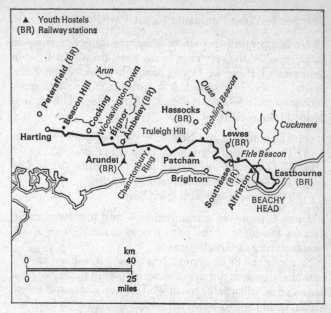

Fig. 34 The South Downs Way

in a series of separate day outings from London. Camping is
not recommended because of the lack of water, but there is
plenty of accommodation en route.

Youth Hostels
Beachy Head, Alfriston, Patcham, Truleigh Hill, Arundel.

Maps
1:50000 sheets 197, 198, 199
1:25000 sheets TV59, TQ50, TQ40, TQ30, TQ31, TQ21,
TQ20, TQ10, TQ11, TQ01, SU91, SU81, SU71

Guides
EASTBOURNE RAMBLING CLUB, *Along the South Downs Way*, 3rd
edn, Eastbourne Rambling Club, 28 Kinfauns Avenue, Eastbourne, Sussex.
TEVIOT, C.J.K., *Walks along the South Downs Way*, 2nd edn, Spurbooks, 1976.

The South-West Peninsula Coast Path

There is a continuous path of some 572 miles following, as far as possible, the very edge of the coast from Minehead in Somerset to Poole in Dorset through some of the finest coastal scenery in England. A description of the route is not necessary as it follows the coast all the way. The path is divided into sections:

(1) The Somerset and North Devon coast path (82 miles)
(2) The Cornwall north coast path (135 miles)
(3) The Cornwall south coast path (133 miles)
(4) The South Devon coast path (146 miles)
(5) The Dorset coast path (76 miles)

There is plenty of accommodation and numerous camp sites on the route of the path but advance booking is advisable during the holiday season.

No special kit or equipment is necessary but shorts are not suitable because of the risk of scratching from thorny vegetation. The weather in the south-west is often warm and sunny which, combined with the salt spray and reflection from the sea, makes for a high sunburn risk.

Youth Hostels
Minehead, Lynton, Instow, Elmscott, Boscastle, Tintagel, Treyarnon Bay, Newquay, Hayle, Land's End, Penzance, Coverack, Pendennis Castle, Boswinger, Golant, Plymouth, Bigbury, Salcombe, Start Bay, Maypool, Beer, Bridport, Litton Cheney, Swanage.

Maps
Somerset and North Devon Coast Path
1:50000 sheets 180, 181, 190
1:25000 sheets SS94, SS84, SS74, SS64, SS54, SS44, SS43, SS42, SS32, SS22, SS21

Cornwall North Coast Path
1:50000 sheets 190, 200, 203, 204
1:25000 sheets SS21, SS20, SX19, SX08, SW97, SW87, SW86, SW75, SW64, SW54, SW53, SW43, SW33, SW32, SW42

Fig. 35 The South-West Peninsula Coast Path

▲ Youth Hostels
(BR) Railway stations

Cornwall South Coast Path
1:50000 sheets 200, 201, 203, 204
1:25000 sheets SW43, SW53, SW52, SW62, SW61, SW71, SW72, SW73, SW83, SW94, SX04, SX05, SX15, SX25, SX35, SX45

Devon South Coast Path
1:50000 sheets 192, 193, 201, 202
1:25000 sheets SX45, SX54, SX64, SX73, SX84, SX85/95, SX86/96, SX97, SX08/18, SY29, SY39

Dorset Coast Path
1:50000 sheets 193, 194, 195
1:25000 sheets SY39, SY49, SY58, SY68, SY67/77, SY78, SY88, SY87/97, SZ07, SZ08

Guides

MARRIOTT, MICHAEL, *The Shell Book of the South-West Peninsula Path*, Queen Anne Press, 1970.

PYATT, EDWARD C., *The South-West Coast Path*, David & Charles, 1971.

RICHARDS, MARK, *Walking the North Cornwall Coastal Footpath*, Thornhill Press, 1975.

SOU'WEST WAY ASSOCIATION, *South-West Way Footpath Information Sheet*, Sou'west Way Association, Beaver Lodge, Rundle Road, Newton Abbot, Devon.

WESTACOTT, H.D., *A Practical Guide to Walking the Devon North Coast Path*, Footpath Publications, Adstock Cottage, Adstock, Buckingham, 1977

WESTACOTT, H. D., *A Practical Guide to Walking the Devon South Coast Path*, 2nd edn., Footpath Publications, Adstock Cottage, Adstock, Buckingham, 1977.

WESTACOTT, H. D., *A Practical Guide to Walking the Dorset Coast Path*, Footpath Publications, Adstock Cottage, Adstock, Buckingham, 1977.

WESTACOTT, H.D., *A Practical Guide to Walking the Cornwall South Coast Path*, Footpath Publications, Adstock Cottage, Adstock, Buckingham, 1977.

Other Long-Distance Paths

There are a number of long-distance routes which have no official backing from the Countryside Commission but which have been cleared and often waymarked by local organizations. Among them are:

The Coast-to-Coast Walk: 190 miles. St Bee's Head, Cumbria, to Robin Hood's Bay.

Footpath Guide
WAINWRIGHT, ALFRED W., *A Coast to Coast Walk. St Bee's Head to Robin Hood's Bay: A Pictorial Guide*, Westmorland Gazette, 1973.

The Cotswold Way: 100 miles. Chipping Camden to Bath.
Footpath Guide
RICHARDS, MARK B., *The Cotswold Way*, Thornhill Press, 1973.

The Crosses Walk: 53 miles across the North York Moors.
Footpath Guide
BOYES, MALCOLM, *The Crosses Walk*, Dalesman, 1974.

The Dales Way: 78 miles. Ilkley to Bowness on Windermere.
Footpath Guides
RAMBLERS' ASSOCIATION, *The Dales Way*, Gerrard Publications, 1970.
SPEAKMAN, COLIN, *The Dales Way*, 2nd edn, Dalesman, 1973.

Hadrian's Wall: 75 miles.
Footpath Guide
HARRISON, DAVID, *Along Hadrian's Wall*, Pan Books, 1972.

Isle of Wight Coastal Path: 60 miles around the island.
Footpath Guide
Available free from the County Surveyor & Planning Officer, County Hall, Newport, Isle of Wight.

London Countryway: 205 miles. Encircles London.
Footpath Guide
CHESTERTON, BRIAN K., *The London Countryway*, Long Distance Walkers' Association, Firle, Chestnut Avenue, Guildford, Surrey.

Lyke Wake Walk: 40 miles across the North York Moors.
Footpath Guide
COWLEY, WILLIAM, *The Lyke Wake Walk*, Dalesman, 1971.

The North Buckinghamshire Way: 32 miles. Chequers Nap to Wolverton.

Footpath Guide
RAMBLERS' ASSOCIATION, *The North Buckinghamshire Way*, Ramblers' Association.

The Peakland Way: 96 miles through the Peak District National Park.

Footpath Guide
MERRILL, JOHN, *The Peakland Way*, Dalesman, 1975.

The Staffordshire Way: 90 miles. Runs from Moir cop to Kinver Edge.

Footpath Guide
Information available from Staffordshire County Council, County Buildings, Stafford.

The Three Peaks Walk

Footpath Guide
GEMMELL, ARTHUR, *The Three Peaks Walk*, Dalesman, 1974.

The Two Moors Way: 103 miles, crossing Dartmoor and Exmoor National Parks.

Footpath Guide
ROWETT, HELEN, *The Two Moors Way*, Devon Ramblers' Association, 46 Langaton Lane, Pinhoe, Exeter EX4 8JX, 1976.

The Viking Way: 150 miles. Runs from Barton-on-Humber to Lincoln.

Footpath Guide
Leaflet available from Lincolnshire County Council, County Offices, Lincoln.

The Wolds Way: 67 miles from North Ferriby to Filey. This is likely to be designated an official long-distance path.

Footpath Guide
RUBINSTEIN, DAVID, *The Wold's Way*, Dalesman, 1972.

Yorkshire Dales Centurion Walk: 100 miles. A circular route through the Yorkshire Dales National Park.

Footpath Guide
GINESI, JONATHAN, *The Official Guidebook to the Yorkshire Dales Centurion Walk*, John Siddall Ltd, Horncastle Street, Cleckheaton, West Yorkshire, 1976.

The following books give details of other long-distance routes:

BERRY, GEOFFREY, *Across Northern Hills: Long-Distance Footpaths in the North of England*, Westmorland Gazette, 1975. Contains routes for the Eden Way (Hawes to near Carlisle, 68 miles); Hadrian's Wall (75 miles); Pennine Link (Ingleborough to Keswick, 70 miles); Roman Way (Ravenglass to Sockbridge, 48 miles).

MOIR, D. G., *Scottish Hill Tracks*, John Bartholomew, 1975, Vol. 1 Southern Scotland; Vol. 2 Northern Scotland. Contains details of over 300 tracks in Scotland which can be linked together to form long-distance routes.

PYATT, EDWARD C., *Chalkways of South and South-East England*, David & Charles, 1974.

STYLES, SHOWELL, *Backpacking in Wales*, Hale, 1977. Contains details of several long-distance routes through Wales.

Scotland contains far more wild and unspoilt countryside
than exists in England and Wales put together. Unfortunately, in recent years some of the country's most beautiful
areas have been put at risk by the discovery of offshore oil
and the need to build terminals and construct drilling plat-
forms. There are also a number of hydro-electric power
stations, but on the whole their effect on the landscape has
not been disastrous. Scotland must have a chapter to itself,
not only because of its very special qualities as a walker's
paradise, but also because walking tends to be a much more
serious undertaking and because there are special problems and difficulties.

There are no national parks in Scotland. This is surprising considering that the country contains some of the most
remote and beautiful countryside in Great Britain. Whereas
in England, and to a lesser extent Wales, a hill-walking expedition almost invariably means visiting a national park,
with all the risk of overcrowding that this involves, this is
not the case in Scotland. Walking in Scotland requires considerably more skill and experience than expeditions to
mountainous areas of England and Wales, not just because
the terrain is more rugged but also because of the remote-
ness and emptiness of much of Scotland and the likely
weather conditions. Route-finding is not only more difficult,
but much more critical, and a certain amount of scrambling
is necessary on some paths. Scrambling is really the most
elementary form of rock-climbing, where roping is not
necessary to keep one's balance. If a walker was taken

secretly to any mountainous area of England and left with a compass but no map, one day's supply of food and proper clothing and boots he could, by noting the direction that the mountains and valleys ran, use his compass to enable him to walk in a straight line and before many hours had passed he would reach a road, farm or settlement. This is not the case in Scotland. The walker's supply of food could easily run out long before he reached a road, let alone a croft or village.

The weather conditions, too, are likely to be much worse even in summer. Wind, mist and heavy rain must be expected, especially in the western parts of Scotland. In winter the conditions can be truly arctic, with temperatures well below zero and winds at times so strong that it is impossible to walk against them. Even in summer the walker can experience blizzards, and snow is likely to lie in some of the corries until June.

It is absolutely essential for every walker to be an expert with map and compass, to leave word with someone responsible and to report safe arrival, never to go alone, to take proper account of weather forecasts and to be ready to turn back if the weather suddenly deteriorates. One of the marks of an experienced walker is that he is prepared to retrace his steps when conditions worsen. The problems of fatigue and hypothermia are immeasurably greater on the Scottish hills than in the rest of Great Britain and when tired and cold it is terrifyingly easy to get into very great danger.

June and September are usually the driest months and June also has the advantage of exceptionally long days. In the north of the country it does not really get dark at all during this month. Eastern Scotland is markedly drier than the west coast. Some towns, including Inverness, average less than 30 ins. of rain per year compared with Loch Quoich's 113 ins. per year.

There are many mountains which will provide the walker with considerable route-finding difficulties. Because the weather is so uncertain the likelihood of walking in thick mist is far greater and frequently survival will depend on the accuracy of one's route-finding. On the way up it is very easy to be tempted on to more and more difficult ground until the way forward demands the skills of a rock-climber and the way back has become dangerous. Sometimes very skilled people have been killed or injured on what are really ordinary, but very narrow paths. Two examples of such paths are those along the summit of An Liathach (3,456 ft) in Glen Torridon and the path from Achnambeithach to the corrie below Stob Coire nan Lochan (3,657 ft) in Glencoe. Both demand care, judgement and a head for heights. But apart from the frequent difficulty of finding the way onto a large and complex mountain or ridge, there is the added need to be sure of finding the right way down. Circular routes are always the most satisfying, but the descent can, and often does, demand more of the walker than the ascent. Glencoe and the Glen Etive both provide good examples of the problem. In Glencoe one of the most rewarding and magnificent mountains to traverse, by a number of different routes, is Bidean nam Bian (3,766 ft). Part of the traverse takes the walker above a lovely corrie called Coire nam Beith, encircled by magnificent rock walls. On a clear day it is obvious that a descent from the ridge by way of this corrie is out of the question for walkers, but in a mist the story is different. From the ridge there are a number of grassy rakes which lead to relatively easy gullies which, in turn, develop into rock walls without warning. Many people who have been tired and cold have tried to descend some of these, frequently with fatal results.

The Ben Starav (3,541 ft) group in Glen Etive provides another example of the trouble a walker can meet. Here the descent from the considerable horseshoe, of which Ben Starav is the first peak, is safely made from one fairly sizable point on Glas Bheinn Mhor (3,258 ft), where the correct route takes the walker to the head waters of Allt Mheuran. But a small error in compass reading will lead the unwary onto a face of steeply sloping boiler-plate slabs. These are difficult to negotiate when dry, but when, as they normally are, they are wet and greasy, they become a death-trap.

In Eastern Scotland, particularly in the Cairngorm range,

problems of another kind are encountered. Here much of the walking in this magnificent country is over what is very like high moorland. Many of the hills are in the 4,000-ft region and are marked by great cliffs, huge gullies and deep glens. The peaks are in general not so well-defined as they are in the west, hence route-finding in bad weather presents obvious difficulties. Far more important than this is the violence of the weather, particularly in the spring and autumn. Blizzards are common, but the combination of rain at an otherwise reasonable temperature with a high wind is an even more serious threat. For the cooling effect of such conditions rapidly leads to hypothermia in the ill-equipped and is one of the commonest causes of mountain deaths in the region.

In describing these dangers it is clear that the line between walking and mountaineering is difficult to draw and that walking in Scotland frequently calls for the all-round skills of the mountaineer. But Scotland can lay some claim to possessing the finest, most beautiful and most exciting terrain that a walker could ever hope to meet.

Sporting Interests

Although the most beautiful parts of Scotland are thinly populated and will support only sheep farming and forestry, it must not be supposed that the land has no other uses. Much of the wilder parts of Scotland belong to large estates, where shooting, fishing and deer-stalking interests are very important. The walker must be aware that huge sums of money are invested in Scottish sporting interests and they play an important part in the tourist industry and thus in the economy of the country.

Walkers have good reason to bless the sportsman because many of the estates have constructed access roads and tracks which have opened up areas of the country which were poorly served by paths. Such tracks and access roads are frequently not rights of way, but walkers are usually permitted to use them, though they may be closed at certain

times during the season. In return for the use of these privileges it is not unreasonable to expect walkers to be meticu-
lous in respecting sporting rights. Walkers can unwittingly
ruin other people's recreation if they cross land on which
stalking or shooting is taking place. During the shooting and
deer-stalking season, which lasts from the beginning of
August until the middle of October, walkers should select
routes which will not interfere with sporting interests. Information about where shooting and stalking is taking place
on particular dates should be obtained locally from the factor's (estate manager's) office, post office, police station,
public house, hotel or Youth Hostel, or from a local person.

Transport

Scotland is very well served by public transport. There is a
rail network which covers most of the country except the
extreme north-west and a remarkably widespread system of
bus routes which seem to link practically every village and
town. Some of these services are operated by local carriers
with no published timetable, so inquiries should be made
locally. Steamer services operate to most of the inhabited
islands and there are air services to some of the larger ones.

Accommodation

One of the curiosities of Scotland is the number of large
hotels often found far from any centre of population. At the
opposite end of the scale, there are camping and caravan
sites and bed and breakfast accommodation available at
some of the crofts. Many of the latter do not advertise and
inquiries should be made locally.

The Scottish Tourist Board has in the last few years introduced the 'Book a bed ahead' scheme. Tourist Information
Centres have been established in numerous towns through
the country, each displaying the 'bed' symbol. Any of these
centres will arrange accommodation, ranging from large
hotels to humble crofts, for visitors on payment of a small fee

and a deposit. When settling the account at the accommodation booked, the deposit is deducted from the bill. This is an invaluable service for travellers and can save many frustrating hours searching for suitable accommodation. There is a good network of Youth Hostels.

It should be noted that in the more modest establishments high tea rather than dinner is more likely to be served. High tea is a splendid Scottish institution consisting of something cooked such as bacon and eggs, sausages or fish followed by bread and butter and jam, scones, cakes and a pot of tea. In terms of both quality and quantity the difference between high tea and dinner to a hungry walker is largely academic.

Rights of Way

As there are no Definitive Maps for Scotland, the Ordnance Survey maps do not distinguish between private and public paths and tracks, although the 1:25000 Outdoor Leisure maps show some routes which have been walked regularly. As has been stated earlier, some paths and tracks have been created for shooting and deer-stalking purposes but as a general rule it will be found that walkers will be allowed to use nearly all paths and tracks marked on the Ordnance Survey, although during the shooting and stalking season inquiries should be made locally. The Scottish Mountaineering Club have issued a series of splendid district guides covering the whole of the country which give a large number of suggested routes. They are not given in detail but provide sufficient information for the walker to mark the route on his Ordnance Survey map. Climbing guides, too, can be useful to the hill-walker as they give details of the route to be followed to reach the climbing area, which is often situated a long way from the nearest road or centre. Such guides are listed under the various Scottish regions below.

The Southern Uplands

Often known as the Lowlands, this area comprises that section of the country lying south of the Glasgow–Edinburgh axis and runs down to the border. Although the term 'Lowlands' is something of a misnomer, as they contain mountains almost as high as any in England, nevertheless this region lacks the rugged quality normally associated with Scottish scenery. The A74 road from Hamilton to Gretna divides the region into two. On the eastern side lies the Border country formed by the river Tweed and its tributaries, where the hills are smooth in outline and covered in grass. On the western side the hills tend to be more rugged in character and generally have a more mountainous appearance. The Southern Uplands are fine walking country but much more akin to the Lake District and Pennines than to the more truly mountainous regions of the rest of Scotland.

RESCUE TEAM
Moffat Hill Rescue Service

MANNED POSTS

Location	*Telephone*
Police Station, Yetholm, Kelso	Kelso 42
Police Station, Moffat	

For rescue go to the rescue post or telephone, whichever is quicker. Dial 999, ask for the police. The position of a post is sometimes changed. Verify locally.

Maps
1:50000 sheets 63, 64, 65, 66, 67, 70, 71, 72, 73, 74, 75, 76, 77, 78, 79, 80, 81, 82, 83, 84, 85, 86, 87

Guidebook
ANDREW, K. M., and THRIPPLETON, A. A., *The Southern Uplands*, Scottish Mountaineering Trust, 1972. (Scottish Mountaineering Club District Guide)
LANGLEY ROBERT, *Walking the Scottish Border*, Hale, 1976.

The Southern Highlands

The Southern Highlands are bounded in the north by the rivers Orchy and Tummel, which form the boundary with the Central Highlands and run down as far south as the Edinburgh–Glasgow axis. They are truly mountainous in character and include Loch Lomond and the Trossachs. As this area lies so close to Scotland's industrial belt it is the most popular walking area in Scotland and its most famous mountains include Ben Lomond, the Cobbler and Ben Lawers.

RESCUE TEAMS

Arrochar MRT
Killin Police Rescue Team
Lomond MRT

MANNED POSTS

Location	Grid Reference	Telephone
Succoth Farm, Arrochar, Argyll	NN 295 053	Arrochar 241
The Hawthorns, Drymen, Stirlingshire	NS 475 886	
Police Station, Crianlarich, Perthshire	NN 387 253	Crianlarich 222
National Trust for Scotland, Visitors Centre Car Park, Ben Lawers (Open Easter–September, daylight hours only)	NN 609 379	Killin 397

UNMANNED POSTS
Scottish Ski Club Hut,
Corrie Odhar, Ben Ghlas,
nr Killin. (No telephone)

For rescue go to the rescue post or telephone, whichever is quicker. Dial 999, ask for the police. The position of a post is sometimes changed. Verify locally.

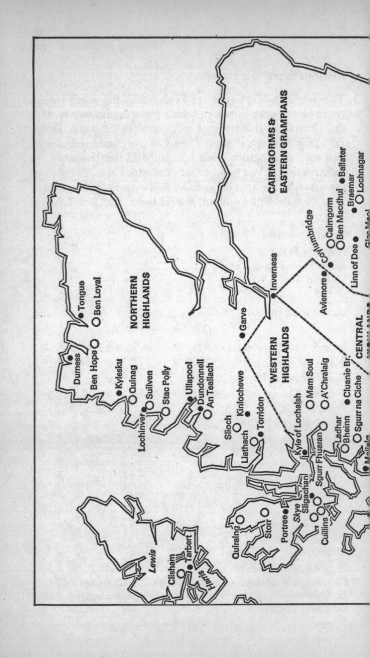

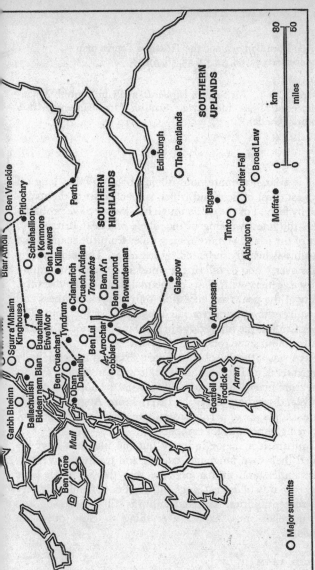

Fig. 36 Scotland

Maps
1:63360 Loch Lomond and the Trossachs Tourist map
1:50000 sheets 49, 50, 51, 52, 55, 56, 57, 58

Guidebook
BENNETT, D. J., *The Southern Highlands*, 2nd edn, Scottish Moun-
   taineering Trust Ltd, 1972. (Scottish Mountaineering Club
   District Guide)

Skye

Skye is a large mountainous island about 60 miles long off
the west coast of Scotland which is reached from the mainland by ferry. For the really tough hill-walker Skye probably
offers the finest walking in the whole of Great Britain. No
part of the island is more than 5 miles from the sea and the
coastline is heavily indented by sea lochs. There are many
peaks over 3,000 ft, offering a wonderful vista of mountain
and sea scenery with views of the mainland in the distance.
Many of the peaks are accessible only to rock-climbers and
all walkers must expect a fair amount of scrambling. The
Black Cuillin, the finest ridge in Scotland, cannot be walked
at all without some rock-climbing.

   Skye has other problems apart from its exceptionally
rugged terrain. The weather is fickle and can vary in a short
time from marvellous to appalling, with the northern end of
the island tending to be the drier. From August onwards
there is a plague of pernicious midges which can prove very
annoying, especially for campers.

   Tourism is a major industry but the islanders have re-
tained their own language, culture and traditions. Visitors
must understand and appreciate that the Skyemen have
their own way of doing things and must not offend their very
real susceptibilities. Sabbatarianism is still very strong and
the traveller must expect everything to close down on
Sunday.

RESCUE TEAM
Skye MRT

MANNED POSTS

Location	Grid Reference	Telephone
Glen Brittle House, Glen Brittle, Skye	NG 411 214	Carbost 232
Police Station, Portree, Skye		Portree 4

UNMANNED POST

Coruisk hut. (No phone. Contains stretcher and first-aid kit)	NG 487 196	

For rescue go to the rescue post or telephone, whichever is quicker. Dial 999, ask for the police. The position of a post is sometimes changed. Verify locally.

Maps
1:50000 sheets 23, 24, 32, 33
1:25000 Cuillin and Torridon Hills Outdoor Leisure map covers part of Skye

Guidebook.
SLESSOR, MALCOLM, *The Island of Skye*, Scottish Mountaineering Trust. (Scottish Mountaineering Club District Guide)

The Western Highlands

The Western Highlands include part of the western sea-board and run north from Loch Linnhe and the Great Glen to a line drawn from the Cromarty Firth along the valleys of the rivers Conon, Bran, and Carron to Loch Carron. The area measures approximately 85 miles from north to south and about 30 miles from west to east. It includes Ardnamur-chan, the most westerly point on the mainland of Great Britain.

The whole area is mountainous, although the mountains in the south are lower than those in the north. There are a number of groups where some of the peaks attain a height of nearly 4,000 ft. Many of the valleys are deep, which makes for steep-sided mountains with pointed summits. This area contains Glen Affric, Glen Cannich and Glen Strathfarrer, which are generally regarded as the three most beautiful glens in all Scotland.

The Western Highlands have few public roads and these follow the coast and the glens. For the experienced hill-walker there is a splendid network of public paths, which will take you through every part of the area.

Unfortunately, this region is one of the wettest areas of Scotland and the walker must expect that on some days of his precious holiday it will be quite impossible to venture onto the mountains.

RESCUE TEAM
Kintail MRT

MANNED POSTS

Location	Grid Reference	Telephone
Police Station, Fort William	NN 101 738	Fort William 2361
Camusrory, Loch Nevis, by Mallaig	NM 857 957	None
The Doctor's House, Tigh-na-Mara, Glenelg, by Kyle	NG 815 194	Glenelg 272
Kintail Lodge Hotel	NG 938 197	Glensheil 275

For rescue go to the rescue post or telephone, whichever is quicker. Dial 999, ask for the police. The position of a post is sometimes changed. Verify locally.

Maps
1:50000 sheets 24, 25, 26, 33, 34, 40, 47, 49

Guidebook
PARKER, JAMES A., *The Western Highlands*, 4th edn, revised by G. Scott Johnstone, Scottish Mountaineering Trust, 1964. (Scottish Mountaineering Club District Guide)

The Central Highlands

The Central Highlands are situated largely in Inverness-shire and Argyll between the Western Highlands and the Cairngorms. The boundary of the region is formed in the south by the Bridge of Orchy, Dalmally and Connel; on the western side by Loch Linnhe and the Great Glen; on the north from Whitebridge to Aviemore and on the east from Aviemore southwards to Dalnacardoch, Kinloch Rannoch and along the railway line to the Bridge of Orchy.

The whole area is mountainous and includes Ben Nevis, at 4,406 ft the highest mountain in Great Britain, as well as several other peaks over 4,000 ft high. There is a good network of paths and it is possible to walk for miles without crossing a road. The Central Highlands has a number of superb ridge walks, one of the most famous being Ben Cruachan.

Ben Nevis itself is a superb viewpoint and in summer can be climbed easily from Fort William or Glen Nevis. In winter, however, it can be very hazardous. Until the beginning of the century there was an observatory and hotel on the summit. Walkers must be prepared for plenty of rain in the Central Highlands. Records from the observatory show that on Ben Nevis in 1898 no less than 240 ins. of rain fell and in December 1900 48 ins. of rain was recorded.

RESCUE TEAMS

Glencoe MRT
Fort William Police Rescue Team
Lochaber Mountain Rescue Association

MANNED POSTS

Location	Grid Reference	Telephone
Achnambeitach, Glencoe	NN 140 566	Ballachulish 311
Kingshouse Hotel, Rannoch Moor, Glencoe, Argyll	NN 260 546	Kingshouse 259

Location	Grid Reference	Telephone
Police Station, Fort William	NN 101 738	Fort William 2361

UNMANNED POSTS

Coire Leis, Ben Nevis, CIC hut. (Direct radio link to police station)	NN 167 723	
Steall, Glen Nevis. (Stretcher only)	NN 177 684	
Scottish Ski Club, Meall Buiridh Hut, Glencoe. (Manned in winter only)	NN 270 520	None

For rescue go to the rescue post or telephone, whichever is quicker. Dial 999, ask for the police. The position of a post is sometimes changed. Verify locally.

Maps
1:63360 Ben Nevis and Glen Coe Tourist map
1:50000 sheets 41, 42, 49, 50, 51

Guidebook
STEVEN, CAMPBELL R., *The Central Highlands*, 3rd edn, Scottish Mountaineering Trust, 1968. (Scottish Mountaineering Club District Guide)

The Northern Highlands

The Northern Highlands include Sutherland, the northern half of Ross-shire and the south-west corner of Caithness. The actual boundary of the region is from Dingwall, Garve and Strath Ban to Achnasheen and westwards to Glen Carron and to the western seaboard.

The area contains some spectacular mountain scenery with a wild and uninhabited hinterland crossed by a number of old drove roads which make for excellent walking. The southern half is made up of Torridonian sandstone, which gives the mountains their characteristic almost archi-

tectural appearance, with rounded and terraced bastions
and ridges with weirdly shaped pinnacles on them.

RESCUE TEAMS
Torridon MRT
Dundonnell MRT

MANNED POSTS

Location	Grid Reference	Telephone
Glen Cottage Hostel, Torridon	NG 930 565	Torridon 222
Dundonnell Hotel, by Garve, Ross-shire	NH 090 881	Dundonnell 204
Inchnadamph Hotel, by Lairg, Sutherland	NC 252 217	Assynt 202
Police Station, Thurso		Thurso 3222

UNMANNED POSTS

Police Station,
Rhiconich, Sutherland.
(First-aid kit and stretcher)

*For rescue go to the rescue post or telephone, whichever is quicker. Dial 999,
ask for the police.* The position of a post is sometimes changed. Verify
locally.

Maps
1:50000 sheets 9, 10, 15, 16, 17, 19, 20, 21, 24, 25, 26
1:25000 Cuillin and Torridon Hills Outdoor Leisure map

Guidebook
STRANG, THOMAS, *The Northern Highlands*, Scottish Mountaineer-
ing Trust, 1970. (Scottish Mountaineering Club District Guide
Book)

The Cairngorms

The Cairngorms should more properly be known as the
Grampians. Cairn Gorm itself (4,084 ft) is only the fourth
highest mountain in the group, yet it has given its name to

this area lying on the eastern side of Scotland between the rivers of Dee and Spey. There is good hill-walking on Cairn Toul (4,241 ft), Braeriach (4,248 ft), Ben Macdui (4,296 ft) and Lochnagar (3,786 ft). Although containing some of the highest land in Great Britain the Cairngorms, especially from a distance, do not give the impression of mountains as do ranges in other parts of Scotland. This is because geologically they are plateaux which have been eroded into mountains, very often giving an unexciting slope on one side with magnificent corries and walls of cliff on the other side.

The Cairngorms have significantly lower rainfall than other mountainous regions of Scotland and even in the highest mountains it does not exceed 60 ins. per year. Extremes of temperature are more likely in this region and the Cairngorms are often warmer in the summer than other parts of Scotland and significantly colder in winter, with a great deal of snow. High winds are much more prevalent than in other parts of the country. Skill with map and compass, and good equipment, are essential.

RESCUE TEAMS

Aberdeen MRT
Braemar Mountain Rescue Association
Cairngorm MRT
Gordonstoun School MRT

MANNED POSTS

Location	Grid Reference	Telephone
Luibeg Cottage, Derry Lodge, Braemar		Braemar 678
Spittal of Muick, Glen Muick, Ballater, Aberdeenshire	NO 307 849	Ballater 530
Police Station, Braemar	NO 148 914	Braemar 222
Police Station, Ballater		Ballater 222
Glenn Doll Lodge, Glen Cova, Angus	NO 278 763	

Location	Grid Reference	Telephone
Aberarder Farm, Lochlagganside, by Newtonmore, Inverness-shire	NN 479 875	Kinlochlaggan 208
Glenmore Lodge, Aviemore, Inverness-shire	NH 986 095	Cairngorm 256
Gordonstoun School, Elgin, Morayshire		Hopeman 445
Police Headquarters, Forfar, Angus		
Police Station, Aviemore, Inverness-shire	NH 895 127	Aviemore 222

UNMANNED POSTS

Location	Grid Reference
White Lady Sheiling, Coire Cas, Cairngorm. (No telephone)	NH 995 053

For rescue go to the rescue post or telephone, whichever is quicker. Dial 999, ask for the police. The position of a post is sometimes changed. Verify locally.

Maps
1:63360 Cairngorms Tourist map
1:50000 sheets 27, 28, 29, 36, 37, 43, 44,
1:25000 High Tops of the Cairngorms Outdoor Leisure map

Guidebook
ALEXANDER, SIR HENRY, *The Cairngorms*, 4th edn, revised by Adam Watson, Scottish Mountaineering Trust, 1968. (Scottish Mountaineering Club District Guide Book)

Bibliography

COUNTRYSIDE COMMISSION FOR SCOTLAND, *Scotland's Countryside*, Countryside Commission for Scotland, Battleby, Redgorton, Perth, 1974.

INGLIS, H. and INGLIS, R., *Hill Path Contours of the Chief Mountain Passes in Scotland*, Gall and Inglis, 1976.

MOIR, D. G., *Scottish Hill Tracks*, No. 1 *Southern Scotland*, No. 2 *Northern Scotland*, John Bartholomew, 1975.

MUNRO, SIR HUGH THOMAS, *Munro's Tables of the 3,000 Feet Mountains of Scotland, and Other Tables of Lesser Height*, Scottish Mountaineering Trust, 1974.

SCOTTISH TOURIST BOARD, *Scotland for Hill Walking*, Scottish Tourist Board, 1975.

14

THE LAW RELATING
TO FOOTPATHS
AND BRIDLEWAYS
IN SCOTLAND

The law relating to rights of way in Scotland is quite different from the law in England. There are no Definitive Maps of rights of way, since 'user' right by the public is based upon custom around which much case law has been built up. It is as well to remember that Scotland has a small population of five million, concentrated for the most part in the lowlands, and there are not the same pressures from recreational interests. There is much wild countryside in its 30,000 square miles, which supports only hill-farming (sheep), forestry, shooting, deer-stalking and fishing and, provided that these interests are not disregarded, walkers enjoy tremendous freedom.

Definitions

In the Countryside (Scotland) Act, 1967 and the Town and Country Planning (Scotland) Act, 1972 the following definitions occur:

Bridleway: A way on which the public have the following but no other rights of way, that is to say, a right of way on foot and a right of way on horseback or leading a horse, with or without a right to drive animals of any description along that way.

Footpath: A way over which the public have the following but no other rights of way, that is to say, a right of way on foot with or without a right of way on pedal cycles.

Public path: A way which is a footpath or bridleway or a combination of those.

Acquisition at Common Law

The majority of public rights of way have been acquired at common law. The criteria for acquiring such rights are as follows:

(1) The path must have been used for the general public for a continuous period of not less than twenty years. The amount of use depends upon local circumstances and a path in thinly populated areas will need less use than a path in a well-populated area.

The use must be by the general public not just by a privileged group such as tenants, employees and postmen. The use must not have been prevented at any time by the landowner such as by closing and locking gates unless it can be shown that the users refused to accept such limitations.

(2) The use must be as a matter of right and not just of toleration or generosity on the part of the landowner.

(3) The beginning and the end of the path must be public places or places where the general public may lawfully resort such as public roads, churches, cemeteries and ferries. It probably includes the summits of the more popular mountains and places on the seashore where the public habitually resort to bathe or for boating.

(4) The path must have a reasonably defined route, though this does not necessarily mean that the track must be visible; but the general public must have always followed approximately the same route and the path must be capable of being used along its whole length.

Acquisition by Statute

Paths may be acquired by statute in a number of ways.

(1) A local planning authority may enter into an agreement with a landowner to create a public path. If it proves

impossible to reach agreement, a path may be created by order. A local planning authority has the power to divert a public path providing that the diversion is not substantially less convenient to the public. Any diversion or creation order has to be confirmed by the Secretary of State for Scotland after objections have been invited. (Countryside (Scotland) Act, 1967, Sections 30, 31 and 38.)

(2) To enable the path network to be maintained the Secretary of State for Scotland may, when making an order extinguishing or diverting a highway to enable development to take place, create or improve other highways. (Town and Country Planning (Scotland) Act, 1972, Sections 198 and 200.)

Similarly, under Section 199 of the same Act, local planning authorities may create or improve other rights of way when making an order extinguishing or diverting public paths to allow development to take place.

Under Section 201 of the Act, orders may be made by the Secretary of State for Scotland if requested by the appropriate local authority to prevent or limit vehicles using a particular highway. There is provision under all these Sections for objections to be made and, if the Secretary of State for Scotland thinks fit, for a local inquiry to be held.

The Secretary of State for Scotland has to confirm all orders made by local authorities unless the order is unopposed.

Enforcement

The Countryside (Scotland) Act, 1967 makes clear provision for the enforcement of the law relating to footpaths and bridleways. Section 46 (i) states: 'It shall be the duty of a local planning authority to assert, protect and keep open and free from obstruction or encroachment any public right of way which is wholly or partly within their area, and they may for these purposes institute and defend legal proceedings and generally take such steps as they may deem expedient.'

Any member of the public may bring an action to vindicate a right of way and this right of vindication includes societies and organizations as well as several persons binding together for this particular purpose.

The legal procedure is by action of declarator that a right of way exists raised in the Sheriff Court or the Court of Session and presenting suitable evidence to prove his point. The kind of evidence required is proof of use as of right for the prescriptive period of twenty years, such as maps, guidebooks and the statements of elderly persons with personal knowledge of the path.

If judgement in favour of the existence of the right of way is given then the question cannot be reopened, but if the judgement is against the existence of a right of way the matter can be reopened if more evidence comes to light.

Maintenance of Public Paths

The landowner of ground crossed by a public right of way has no responsibility for maintaining or repairing the route. The public may repair a right of way providing that no damage is caused to the landowner's property. Under Section 46 of the Countryside (Scotland) Act, 1967 local planning authorities have a duty to assert, protect, keep open and free from obstruction or encroachment any public right of way within their area. This section gives local planning authorities power to maintain paths if they so wish but they are under no obligation to do so. However, under Section 33 of the same Act, local planning authorities have a duty to maintain public paths which have been created by agreement or order or diversion orders. The Secretary of State for Scotland has the power to order local planning authorities to carry out necessary work if he thinks they have failed in their duty.

Guideposting

Guideposts may be erected by local authorities upon any right of way and, under Section 46 of the Countryside (Scotland) Act, 1967, by any person with the consent of the local planning authority. Section 53 of the same Act permits local authorities to make a financial contribution to anyone carrying out such work.

Diversion of Paths

A landowner has no right to alter the route without due legal process, although there is usually no difficulty if the public using the route accept any minor changes as reasonable.

The procedure to divert the path is for the landlord, tenant or occupier of the land crossed by the path to apply to the local planning authority for a diversion order. The planning authority must invite objections to the diversion and then make a diversion in the light of the circumstances. (Countryside (Scotland) Act, 1967, Section 35.)

(1) A local planning authority may make a diversion order extinguishing a right of way and substituting a new right of way providing that the new path is not substantially less convenient for the public. Any such orders have to be considered in the light of objections made and the order has to be confirmed by the Secretary of State for Scotland. (Countryside (Scotland) Act, 1967, Section 38.)

(2) A bridleway, which includes public paths, may be diverted by the Secretary of State for Scotland to allow development after objections have been invited. (Town and Country Planning (Scotland) Act, 1972, Section 198.)

(3) Local planning authorities may divert paths to allow development to take place after inviting objections and obtaining confirmation, if necessary, by the Secretary of State for Scotland. (Town and Country Planning (Scotland) Act, 1972, Section 199.)

Extinction of Paths

(1) Paths acquired by common law may be extinguished if they have not been used for twenty years providing that the general public have acquiesced in this disuse. Common-law extinguishment needs no positive action on the part of the landowner, but of course it is possible to challenge the extinguishment in the courts.

(2) All public paths, whether acquired by statute or at common law, may be the subject of extinguishment orders.

(3) Local authorities and certain statutory bodies such as Electricity Boards have the power to acquire land free of all rights of way.

(4) Local planning authorities have the power to extinguish a right of way on the grounds that it is not needed for public use by means of a public path extinguishment order which has to be submitted to the Secretary of State for Scotland for confirmation. (Countryside (Scotland) Act, 1967, Section 34.)

(5) The Secretary of State for Scotland may issue an order extinguishing any right of way if the land crossed by the right of way has been acquired for planning purposes by the local authority. He must be satisfied that an alternative right of way has been provided, will be provided or is not necessary.

A local authority may extinguish a footpath or bridleway on the same grounds and conditions. (Town and Country Planning (Scotland) Act, 1972.)

Obstructions

Obstructions of any kind that are likely to impede the person using the path are not permitted on rights of way. Such obstructions include barbed wire, electric fences, walls and fences unless provided with proper access such as a gate or stile. Bridleways must not have stiles placed on them and it is illegal to lock a gate on any public right of way.

Anyone wishing to erect a stile or gate across a public

right of way must apply to the planning authority for permission to do so. If the planning authority refuses permission the applicant may appeal to the Secretary of State for Scotland. (Countryside (Scotland) Act, 1967, Section 45.)

The remedy for a walker meeting an obstruction on a public right of way is to remove as much of it as necessary to allow him to pass. The law recognizes this right providing that the action is taken within a reasonably short time of the erection of the obstruction. Obstructions which cannot be dealt with in this manner should be brought to the notice of the local planning authority for action as described above under 'Enforcement'.

Ploughing

Landowners and tenants have a right to plough public paths unless this right has been excluded by a public path creation agreement or order or a diversion order. The landowner or tenant must inform the local planning authority within seven days of ploughing the right of way and must reinstate the surface as soon as may be. Although the public have the right to continue to use paths that have been ploughed (Countryside (Scotland) Act, 1967, Section 43), commonsense dictates, in most cases, walking round the edges of fields.

Bulls

The law concerning bulls on public paths is confused. It is an offence to permit a bull of a recognized dairy breed over ten months old to be at large in a field crossed by a public path unless cows or heifers are also at large in the same field (Countryside (Scotland) Act, 1967, Section 44). However, it is believed that under common law it is illegal to have any bull running free in a field crossed by a public right of way, although to prove the point a case would have to be heard in the courts.

Maps

Although there are no Definitive Maps in Scotland, local authorities have, in some cases, prepared lists of rights of way and maps, but although these may be challenged their publication helps towards the establishment of rights of way by use by the public.

(1) The Secretary of State for Scotland must prepare maps of the Scottish Countryside excluding burghs of 5,000 inhabitants or more. (Countryside (Scotland) Act, 1967, Section 26.)

(2) Local planning authorities have a duty to prepare and keep up to date maps showing details of any land which has been acquired for public access or which has been made subject to access agreements (Countryside (Scotland) Act, 1967, Section 26). Local planning authorities must record details of all orders for access, creation, diversion and extinguishment of paths on maps.

Access to the Countryside

Under the provisions of the Countryside (Scotland) Act, 1967, various authorities are empowered to establish rights of access in the countryside. A right of access is not the same as establishing a right of way – it can be better compared to the enjoyment of a public park. It also produces a negative right in that one cannot be treated a trespasser when acting lawfully. Access agreements are not usually applied to 'excepted land', which includes agricultural land.

Local planning authorities may establish country parks or pleasure grounds and administer them for the benefit of the public. (Countryside (Scotland) Act, 1967, Section 48.)

The Forestry Commission may establish recreational facilities, including nature trails and paths. (Countryside (Scotland) Act, 1967, Section 58.)

The Secretary of State for Scotland may establish recreational facilities, including nature trails and paths on land owned by the government and may appoint the Countryside Commission for Scotland as his agent. (Countryside (Scotland) Act, 1967, Section 60.)

A local planning authority may, with the approval of the Secretary of State for Scotland, negotiate access agreements with landowners and others having interest in the land such as holders of fishing and shooting rights. Rights of way shall not be affected by the terms of access agreements. If it proves impossible to conclude an agreement, the planning authority may make a compulsory access order, which has to be approved by the Secretary of State after hearing objections before the order can become effective. (Countryside (Scotland) Act, 1967, Sections 13 and 14.)

If it proves impossible to provide access either by agreement or by making an order, the planning authority may with the consent of the Secretary of State for Scotland acquire the land either by agreement or compulsorily. (Countryside (Scotland) Act, 1967, Section 24.)

The Secretary of State for Scotland may acquire land by agreement, or compulsorily, if it has proved impossible to provide access either by agreement or by order. (Countryside (Scotland) Act, 1967, Section 25.)

How to Preserve Rights of Way

The body most active in the preservation of rights of way is the Scottish Rights of Way Society Limited, which will offer advice and, where necessary, approach the proper authorities. An individual who comes across problems should take up the matter with the landowner, or if this produces no result with the local planning authority, asking them to take action under Section 46 of the Countryside (Scotland) Act, 1967 'to assert, protect, and keep open and free from obstruction or encroachment any right of way'. Should these approaches fail, the Scottish Rights of Way Society should be informed, giving a clear description of the problem together with a grid reference.

Members of the public can help, too, just by walking

paths which are in danger of falling into disuse. This will help prevent losing those paths subject to common law under the prescriptive period of twenty years.

The philosophy behind the preservation of rights of way in Scotland is quite different from the English concept. The law is dynamic and paths that have fallen into disuse because they no longer serve a useful purpose are replaced by new paths which may become rights of way in twenty years' time.

Bibliography

Rights of Way – A Walker's Guide to the Law of Right of Way in Scotland, revised edn, Scottish Rights of Way Society Ltd, 32 Rutland Square, Edinburgh EHI 2BZ, 1972.

15

SAFETY, THE
WEATHER AND
OTHER MATTERS

In Chapter 2, discussing clothing and equipment for walking in the high places, I wrote about the dangers of exposure and how quickly one can die if not properly equipped. I described the case of a man who had died in a few hours after his tent had blown down on a mild night in early September. By contrast, there was a case in the winter of 1974-5 when a fifteen-year-old schoolboy got lost on the fells above Grassington in Yorkshire. Fortunately, he was properly equipped with plenty of food, a stove and plastic survival bag. He survived no less than four freezing February nights before being found none the worse for his experience. Undoubtedly, he should not have set out on such a walk alone in winter, but when things went wrong he kept his head and remembered all the survival techniques he had been taught.

Everyone venturing onto the fells must be aware that there is an element of danger. It is the height of folly to go unless properly dressed and equipped with map and compass. Only the experienced should walk alone. Careful note should be taken of the weather forecast and, if visibility is likely to be poor, it is better not to go. Even with the most careful preparations things can still go wrong. An ankle can be twisted, a compass can be broken or lost, a map blown away in the wind. If misfortunes like these happen in fog, the lone walker can be in real trouble. All fell-walkers should have some knowledge of survival techniques so that if they do get into trouble they know exactly what to do. In every rucksack should be carried a spare woollen sweater, woollen gloves, a large plastic survival bag or 'space blanket', plenty of spare food, a torch and first-aid kit containing Elastoplast for blisters, a couple of dressings and six triangular bandages. If you have a first-aid certificate you will be able to cope with most emergencies.

If trouble does occur, the first thing to do is try to find a sheltered spot such as a shepherd's hut, the lee of a stone wall, a sink hole or some deep depression in the heather. Put on all the clothes in the rucksack, cut a mouth hole in the plastic survival bag and pull it over the head, first pulling up the anorak hood. Try to find something to act as an insulator to sit on such as a thick mattress of heather. Empty the rucksack and put your feet, with your boots still on, into it, carefully arranging the rucksack under the skirt of the survival bag. Lastly, slip your arms out of the sleeves of your anorak as this will help to keep you warm. Stay like this until conditions improve or help arrives. If you really need help, blow your whistle using the international mountain distress signal of six blasts repeated at minute intervals.

A group of people should huddle together and, if very cold, take it in turns to sit on the outside of the circle. Only if someone is injured should the group break up and attempt to go for help and, ideally, at least three of the party should set out together.

Exposure

Exposure or hypothermia is probably the greatest danger in the mountains. It is caused by the body surface being chilled sufficiently long for the body core temperature to be lowered to a point where it can no longer maintain the vital organs. When the skin and the tissues immediately below it become cold, blood rushes to the surface to warm the affected area. If it is very cold, the blood itself is cooled and returns to the body core to be warmed again. If this process goes on for long it will quickly sap the energy of the patient and result in death. One of the most significant factors in exposure is the strength of the wind, which causes what is known as the 'wind-chill factor' shown diagramatically in Figure 37.

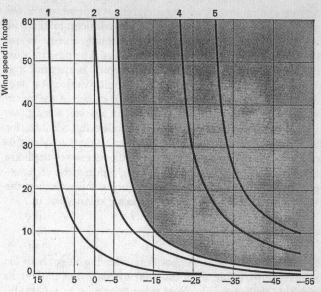

Fig. 37. Wind-chill scale

Line 1 indicates when the temperature feels cold

Line 2 indicates when the temperature feels bitterly cold

Line 3 indicates when flesh exposed to the air is likely to freeze

Line 4 indicates when flesh exposed to the air is liable to freeze in one minute

Line 5 indicates when flesh exposed to the air is liable to freeze in thirty seconds.

The shaded area indicates when conditions are dangerous to survival.

It will be appreciated from the diagram that a person standing in still air at −25° C. is no more at risk than someone wearing similar clothes standing in a 30-knot wind when the temperature is 10° C.

Exposure can be avoided in most weather conditions by wearing the proper clothing. The risk is accentuated by fatigue and hunger. Unfortunately, the symptoms of the onset of exposure are not very striking, and difficult to diagnose in oneself. The danger signals are stumbling, a sense of unreality and difficulty in making decisions. The patient must be given rest, warmth and food. Warmth is essential and serious cases should be treated by wrapping in sleeping bags or blankets, preferably with another member of the party whose body heat will help the patient. Never attempt to impart warmth by rubbing or administering alcohol, for although spirits make a person feel warm they achieve this by encouraging the blood to go from the recesses of the body to the surface, which has the effect of sending the cool surface blood into the body, thus reducing even further the body core temperature. Rubbing has a similar effect.

Mountain Rescue

Should you ever be in the position of having to get help for someone in trouble, it is essential to make the patient as comfortable as possible. Next mark your map as accurately as you can, showing the position of the patient. Examine the map carefully to work out the quickest way of getting help. It might be quicker to head across country to the nearest road to stop a car, or there might be a farm at the head of a near-by valley, although not all farm buildings marked on the map are necessarily inhabited. Make your plan and reassure the patient by telling him of your intentions. Get to a telephone as soon as possible, dial 999 and ask for the police, as they normally co-ordinate rescue services. Keep calm, give details of the patient together with a description of his position, including a grid reference. Answer carefully and precisely all the questions the police put to you. It is quite likely that you will be asked if you are willing to accompany the rescue party in order to show them the exact position of the injured person. Most people want to go immediately, but you should consider very carefully whether you are in a fit condition. Remember that mountain rescue teams are made up of very fit men and they will want to travel fast.

Note carefully any instructions the police may give you and obey them meticulously. Naturally you will be very concerned about the patient and very conscious of the passing of time. It takes some time to get together the eight or ten men of the mountain rescue team, as they are all volunteers and have to be called from their place of work. If you do return with them, it is quite likely that you will have to take your turn on the stretcher party. Handling a stretcher in mountainous country is very hard work. Six stretcher bearers are needed – one at each end and two on each side. The front and rear bearers have a full harness and the four side bearers have a webbing strap which passes over the shoulders. One hand holds the stretcher and the other holds the strap so that much of the weight is taken on the shoulders. On narrow rocky mountain paths the language tends to be picturesque!

Mountain rescue services are provided free in Great Britain and are often made up of volunteers who undertake such work for love of their fellow men. They have to spend hours, sometimes even days, searching, often in bad weather, for walkers and climbers who, more often than not, have got into difficulties because of their own foolhardiness. Some of these volunteers actually lose wages as a result of their rescue activities. Remember, then, if ever you have to be rescued to make a handsome donation to the work of the rescue team who perhaps saved your life.

Blisters

Fortunately, comparatively few people have to be rescued each year, but probably thousands of others require some simple first aid. Blisters are the commonest cause of discomfort in walkers. Prevention is better than cure and the point has to be made that blisters would not develop if the proper precautions were taken. At the first hint of a blister stop and examine the foot. If there is a small blister, sterilize a needle in a match flame and gently push the needle through the blister from one side to the other. Take a clean tissue and gently squeeze the blister until all the fluid is out. From the first-aid kit select a suitable-sized cushioned plaster and cut away the medicated gauze (this is to prevent the hard gauze aggravating the trouble). Gently press the plaster into place and smooth it into position. Try to establish the cause of the blister by examining socks and boots for any foreign matter. More severe blisters should be protected by thick adhesive moleskin. Carefully cut a hole in the moleskin large enough to contain the blister. Apply the moleskin after piercing the blister, then cover the hole with an ordinary plaster with the gauze removed. This technique will effectively remove all further pressure from the blister.

Sunburn and Windburn

A hot summer's day brings with it the risk of sunburn. On the fells it is not often that the wind is still enough for the walker to want to expose much of his body except perhaps his arms, but in the lowland country there is a temptation to bare the arms and legs. Exercise increases the risk of sunburn because perspiration tends to irritate the skin made tender by the sun. The damage is often done before the sufferer realizes that he is being affected and therefore it is advisable to be aware of the danger and to keep the limbs covered by light clothing.

Windburn is more common than sunburn in the high places and usually makes the face tender and cracks the lips. It is sensible to carry a soothing cream and some lip salve.

Emergency Rations

All walkers should carry a reasonable supply of food and drink. It is unwise to rely on pubs even in lowland areas because there is always the risk of being delayed, or the food being sold out before arriving. It is extremely foolish not to carry food and water on the fells. In addition to the food needed for the day, emergency rations must be carried. Take what you enjoy eating but ideally it should be rich in protein. I always take crispbread and cheese, dates and apples. The emergency rations should include more crispbread and cheese, dates, fruit, Kendal Mint Cake and chocolate. Probably the most refreshing drink is lemon or lime (or beer if you can get it!). Avoid all carbonated drinks or you will find that you will regret drinking them for several hours afterwards. Find room in the rucksack for a tube of water-purifying tablets so that in an emergency mountain water can be drunk.

The Weather

The weather is an unfailing topic of conversation in all parts of Great Britain. Owing to its location in a great ocean off a very large landmass, our country experiences very unsettled weather and surprising variations in the amount of rainfall. According to the *Guinness Book of Records* the wettest place is Styhead Tarn in Cumbria, with a mean average rainfall of 172·9 ins. per year, and the driest is Great Wakering in Essex, with a mean average rainfall of 19·2 ins. per year.

As most of our rain is brought by westerly and south-westerly winds and because there is much high land in the western part of the country it follows that the eastern parts of the country are much drier than the western parts. For example, Edinburgh's mean average rainfall is 27·5 ins. compared with 39 ins. for Glasgow. There can be enormous variations locally, for example Grasmere has 95 ins. of rain each year whereas Windermere, which is only eight miles away, has only 68 ins. and Seathwaite, seven miles from Grasmere, has 131 ins. each year.

Generally speaking, the walker is more interested in the absence of adverse conditions than in sunny weather. Firm rules cannot be laid down for selecting the best time to take a walking holiday but the weather records show that

June and September are often the driest months, with a good chance of fine sunny spells at the beginning of both months. July and August are usually wetter than the other summer months.

The country is well covered by the national weather forecast which is broadcast on radio and television. In addition, local forecasts are available by telephone and details will be found in all telephone directories. When camping it is not always possible or convenient to telephone the weather service and many campers use a small transistor radio for receiving forecasts.

It is very useful to be able to anticipate changes in the weather and to interpret correctly what the wind and clouds are signalling. Providing they are understood properly, there is truth in some of the old-fashioned weather proverbs.

'Red sky at night, shepherd's delight' is nearly always true if the red sky is caused by the rays of the setting sun reflected on clouds very high in the sky, indicating that a cold front has just passed and that there will now be a period of settled weather.

'Rain before seven, fine by eleven' is very often found to be correct because, unless the depression is very deep, indicated by very thick, fast-moving, low-lying stratus clouds, it rarely rains for more than four hours at a stretch in Great Britain.

'Red sky at morning, shepherd's warning' is usually true when the sun's rays are shining on high clouds which signals the approach of a warm front which will bring rain with it.

In summer time if the day dawns crystal clear with the hardness of a sapphire then the weather is certain to deteriorate within a few hours.

There is one virtually foolproof method known as the 'cross-wind rule' of establishing whether the weather will deteriorate or improve within a few hours. It is often not appreciated that weather conditions cause winds to blow in different directions at certain heights. Thus the clouds may move in a direction different from that of the surface wind which the observer can feel on his face.

Rule 1: Stand with your back to the surface wind and if the clouds come from the *left*-hand side then the weather will usually deteriorate in the next few hours.

Rule 2: Stand with your back to the surface wind and if the clouds come from the *right*-hand side then the weather will usually improve within the next few hours.

Rule 3: Stand with your back to the surface wind and if the clouds move on a parallel course the weather will not change very much during the next few hours.

(The walker must ensure that his back is turned towards the true surface wind and that the direction has not been distorted by natural features such as mountains and hills.)

The Mountain Code

In this chapter and throughout the book great emphasis has been laid on the need to follow a safe code of conduct when walking in the high places. It must not be thought that there is danger lurking behind every cairn or in every mountain stream; but as with almost any sport or recreation there is an element of risk which is greatly increased by foolhardiness. Always follow the mountain code:

Be Prepared

Do not tackle anything which is beyond your training and experience.

Ensure that your equipment is sound.

Know the rescue facilities available in the area you are in and the procedure in case of accidents.

Know first aid.

Avoid going into the mountains alone unless you are very experienced.

Leave word of your route and proposed time of return. Always report your return.

Make sure your map and compass skills are well practised. Rely on your compass.

Consider Other People
Avoid game-shooting parties.
Lead only climbs and walks which you are competent to lead.
Enjoy the quiet of the countryside; loud voices and radios do
    disturb.
Do not throw stones and dislodge boulders.
Do not pollute water.
Choose a climb which will not interfere with others, or wait
    your turn.

Be Weather Wise
Know the local weather forecast.
Weather conditions change rapidly. Do not hesitate to turn
    back.
Know the conditions on the mountain; if there is snow or ice
    only go out when you have mastered the use of ice axe and
    rope.

Respect the Land
Keep to footpaths through farm and woodland. If in doubt,
    ask.
Camp on official sites or obtain permission of the landowner.
Dig a hole to make a latrine and replace the turf.
Remember the danger of starting a fire.
Take all your litter home.
Avoid startling sheep and cattle.

Help Conserve Wild Life
Enjoy the plants, flowers and trees but never remove or
    damage them.
Avoid disturbing wild life.

I nearly always walk alone, as I prefer my own company
in the mountains – I find that companions rarely share my
brand of ecstasy. I like to talk to myself and am constantly
astonished at the wit, perspicacity and shrewdness of my
replies! Nor do I leave word with anyone of where I am
going. This is because I carry enough food and equipment

to last two or three days, and as I always have a map and compass I feel that the only ill luck that could befall me is that of accidental injury. There are some who will read this and 'tut tut' disapprovingly. No doubt they are right, but the mountains, together with the sea, remain one of the few places where one can feel a sense of freedom and the wonder and joy of being a man pitting yourself against nature and the elements – a struggle which is heightened by the magnificent surroundings. No, I cannot be bound by all the rules but insist to the novice that only the truly experienced walker can afford to break any of them.

Bibliography

BROWN, T., and HUNTER, R., *Spurbook of Outdoor First-Aid*, Spurbooks, 1976.

BROWN, T., and HUNTER, R., *Spurbook of Survival and Rescue*, Spurbooks, 1976.

JACKSON, JOHN, and others, *Safety on Mountains*, revised edn, British Mountaineering Council, 1975.

LANGMUIR, ERIC, *Mountain Leadership Handbook: The Official Handbook of the Mountain Leadership Training Boards of Great Britain*, Scottish Council of Physical Recreation, 1971.

MACINNES, HAMISH, *The International Mountain Rescue Handbook*, Constable, 1972.

METEOROLOGICAL OFFICE, *Averages of Rainfall for Great Britain and Northern Ireland, 1916–1950*, HMSO, 1958.

METEOROLOGICAL OFFICE, *British Rainfall*, HMSO, published annually; 1968 is the latest year available.

MOUNTAIN RESCUE COMMITTEE, *Mountain and Cave Rescue*, Mountain Rescue Committee, 1970.

PAULCKE, WILHELM, *Hazards in Mountaineering*, Kaye & Ward, 1973.

WATTS, ALAN, *Instant Weather Forecasting*, Adlard Coles, 1968.

Footpath guides serve a number of purposes. Firstly, it is
reasonable to assume that the author knows the area well
and has chosen the best routes and therefore they are useful
for recommending routes. Secondly, they supplement maps
and in many cases provide more detailed information than
the Ordnance Survey map, though experienced walkers
usually like to have the appropriate Ordnance Survey map
with them even when using a footpath guide. Thirdly, they
are extremely useful to the many people who enjoy a walk
in the countryside but to whom the Ordnance Survey map
is something of a mystery. Footpath guides are usually devoted to a particular area, but in recent years a number of
guides to long-distance footpaths have been published, some
of which cover considerable stretches of contrasting countryside.

There are two distinct categories of footpath guides. Illustrative, where the main emphasis is on drawing maps sufficiently detailed for the walker to follow the path, and
descriptive, where the author gives a description of the route
supplemented either by sketch maps or by superimposing
the line of the path on the Ordnance Survey map.

Illustrative Guides

The best-known examples of illustrative guides are A. Wainwright's seven *Guides to the Lakeland Fells*. These contain superb maps on a scale of 1 :25000, giving details not found on
Ordnance Survey maps such as gates, stiles, cairns and indi-

vidual trees for all routes to the summit of every mountain and fell in the Lake District. In addition, they contain delightful line drawings and an entertaining, but erudite, commentary on things to be seen along the route. Mr Wainwright has set a standard that few can emulate, although the principles that he uses can be applied to any area. Mark Richards has done a superb guide to the North Cornwall Coastal Footpath, adopting the methods used by Mr Wainwright in his *Pennine Way Companion*.

An interesting development in footpath guides is the Automobile Association *No Through Road*. This is a large coffee-table item with a separate book of walks in a ring binder. These selected walks cover the whole country but are very short. What is so interesting is that the routes are shown by means of coloured aerial photographs. This method seems very effective but is so expensive that the technique can be used only for books which will have a huge sale.

Descriptive Guides

Descriptive guides vary greatly in quality and usefulness. It is very difficult to write accurate descriptions of a route and only the most skilful writer will manage to avoid ambiguities. The countryside is constantly changing and if, for example, a farmer embarks on some alterations or improvements to his land it can render a descriptive guide useless. For example, 'after passing through the stile, walk up the track and take the third gate on the right-hand side' is apparently clear and unambiguous, but what if the farmer decides on an alteration to his fields and either removes one of the gates and fills the gap with fencing, or substitutes a stile for which the walker is looking? With a good illustrative guide, the changes would not be so confusing because the walker would have a very clear idea of how far he had to walk before reaching the gate and there should be other features such as field boundaries to help him identify the route. Nevertheless, good descriptive guides can be perfectly adequate in uncultivated country, where there is little likelihood of significant changes and where the paths and tracks are clearly defined, and are preferred by those who lack confidence in map-reading.

Writing a Footpath Guide

There is a great demand for footpath guides. The market for them in popular walking areas is considerable (countless thousands of Mr Wainwright's guides have been sold) and there is a great demand from local people in areas which have no special scenic qualities and which are unlikely to be visited by many walkers from outside the area. The publication of a footpath guide is a sure recipe for getting local paths walked and if done by a rambling club can provide a useful addition to club funds. It can also become a fascinating hobby.

Careful consideration should be given to the kind of guide required and the principles on which it should be compiled. Illustrative guides may either be comprehensive, giving the route of every path and details of gates, stiles, trees, fences, telegraph poles etc. to be found in each field crossed by a path, or they may be selective, using the same principles but just giving a few walks. Experience shows that circular walks of about five miles are the most popular with the general public. If, from each starting point, two walks are always given, this will cater for those who like to walk a longer distance.

Much thought must be given to the information to be included in the guide. In lowland areas, the most important features are field boundaries, roads and streams. It is helpful to indicate the kind of field boundary, whether it be hedge, post and rail fence or barbed wire, and any other permanent features such as barns, pylons and telegraph poles. Unless your calligraphy is superb it will be found easier to indicate stiles, gates, footpath and bridleway signs by single letters rather than writing them out in full. Once these decisions have been made, it is sensible to compile the key to the finished map to ensure consistency throughout. Most good reference libraries have a number of footpath guides in their collection and the would-be cartographer can pick up some useful ideas by examining them.

Surveying

Every path must be surveyed and this will involve you in a great deal of work and walking. A book containing twenty circular five-mile walks adds up to a minimum of one hundred miles. In addition, it will be necessary to note any difficulties such as missing footbridges and stiles, locked gates, obstructions etc., and take them up with the landowner or responsible local authority, which will result in further visits to check that the work has been done. The work involved in producing a comprehensive guide to fifteen or so parishes is very great. Obviously, the density of the path network varies considerably in different parts of the country, but if my experience, based on parishes in north Buckinghamshire, is typical then there are likely to be between ten and fifteen miles of public path per parish. I have found that my guides contain about two hundred miles of path and that I walk about four hundred miles to survey each one and check that obstructions are removed and missing footbridges are replaced.

The following items are required for surveying:

    clipboard
    2 H pencil attached to the clipboard by nylon cord
    pencil sharpener
    eraser
    relevant map

The clipboard can be improved by gluing some ¼-in. plastic angle moulding obtainable from a hardware shop to the edges to form a frame. A piece of thick flexible transparent plastic will protect the map on the clipboard from sweaty hands and a large transparent plastic bag will protect the clipboard from the rain. The map used should be the 1:25000, preferably the outline edition which omits contours. Mark in rights of way using the Definitive Map, where available, checking with the appropriate authority that there are no diversions or extinguishments. Next, walk the chosen route marking the map as you go with all the features you intend to include, not forgetting to amend the map where development has now rendered it inaccurate. It will not be possible for you to locate the additional features you require with complete accuracy. Nevertheless, with a little experience you will find how easy it is to line up telegraph poles and pylons with other physical features and then to estimate the distance they lie from one of these features. It is a great help to know the exact number of normal walking paces you take to cover one hundred metres. Use a surveyor's tape to measure the distance and then walk it ten times counting your paces. It is likely that the number of paces will vary each time so take the average figure. Once this information is known, you will find it easy to judge distances by counting your steps and measuring short distances on the map with the help of a romer scale or the rule on the base of a Silva compass.

Drawing the Map

Once the survey is completed, the final map can be drawn. The following items will be necessary:

> drawing board
> T-square
> 4 drawing-board clips
> Rotring micronorm pen with 0·25-mm. nib
> Rotring black drawing ink
> Rotring pen cleaner
> studio gum
> Snopake correcting fluid
> best-quality tracing paper
> graph paper
> Letraset

Mount the map on the drawing board using studio gum if

necessary, and hold the tracing paper on the drawing board with the four clips. In pencil mark out the size of the page and then, within this border, make a tracing of the map and features to be included. If the guide is to be a club venture, it may be possible to find a draughtsman or someone with similar skills to draw and letter the map. Most people, with a little patience and practice, can learn to letter acceptably, for neatness and a personal style is more important than perfect proportions. Books on lettering and calligraphy can be obtained from the public library. When lettering, it is helpful to mount the tracing paper on graph paper as this will help to get the lettering straight and properly proportioned. The plates for printing can be made direct from the traced maps but for ease of handling it is better to mount them with studio gum on best-quality bond typing paper. The wording on the cover and the heading on each map can be done with Letraset and a small line drawing on the cover will help to make it attractive and eyecatching.

Legal Requirements

Before printing the guide, there are certain legal requirements to be met. Application must be made to The Director General, Ordnance Survey, Maybush, Southampton, for permission to publish a guide based on the Ordnance Survey maps. A form will have to be completed and a copyright fee paid before publication. The Ordnance Survey find it helpful if photocopies of the maps are enclosed with the copyright forms. The copyright fee is now considerable and inquiries should be made before much work is done on the guide. The Ordnance Survey require the words 'Crown copyright reserved' to appear on every map and an acknowledgement to appear in the book: 'The maps in this guide are based upon the Ordnance Survey maps with the sanction of the Controller of HM Stationery Office. Crown copyright reserved.'

At this stage it is a good plan to write to J. Whitaker & Sons Ltd, 13 Bedford Square, London WC1, asking to be assigned an International Standard Book Number. ISBNs are used in the book trade for identifying books and it should appear in the book in the appropriate place. Request also a *Whitaker Information Form* which will ensure that the book is listed in *The Bookseller* and *British Books in Print*. *The Bookseller* is a weekly trade publication used extensively by booksellers and librarians and *British Books in Print* is an annual publication listing all British books in print. This service is free. By law, a copy of the book must be sent free to The British Library Bibliographical Services Division, Store Street, London WCIE 7DG. This copy will be added to the stock of the British Library (formerly the British Museum Library) and will appear under author, title and subject in the British National Bibliography, a book used extensively by librarians for tracing books and information. In the course of time an entry will appear in the printed catalogue of the British Library. The Crown Agent has the right to demand, free of charge, an additional four copies, one each for the university libraries of Oxford and Cambridge, the National Library of Scotland and the Library of Trinity College, Dublin.

Printing

For the reproduction of maps, the most suitable process is undoubtedly offset lithography, involving some form of photographic plate. The advantage of this method is that mistakes in the copy can be painted over with correcting fluid and redrawn without having to start the whole map afresh. Although the finished copy may look a mess, all the imperfections will disappear in the photographic process. Another advantage of using a photographic method is that the copy can be enlarged or reduced to fit the page. This is particularly useful for printing any text which may go in the guide, as it can be typed on a page larger than the finished product and then reduced in the plate-making process, thus saving space and also producing a more acceptable result.

Although it is possible to print in colour, the cost is prohibitive and the guide should be produced in monochrome. Prices vary considerably and it is wise to obtain quotations from several firms listed in the Yellow Pages under Printers & Lithographers. As an indication of the prices, 1,000 copies of a twenty-four page publication (i.e. twelve sheets backed, which includes the cover) on A5 paper will cost in the region of £120 using the negative and plate method which will give the best result. If paper masters are used, the price is likely to be about £80, but the result will not be nearly so satisfactory as the definition will be much less sharp. Firms advertising instant lithographic printing will usually be found to be prohibitively expensive.

Marketing and Distribution

When the book is published, a press release describing the book, its main features and its purpose should be sent with a copy of the book to editors of all local newspapers and to the local radio station. Both media are usually keen to review local material. Footpath guides are reviewed in *The Rucksack*, the journal of the Ramblers' Association, and orders are likely to come from all over the country. Send copies, too, to any local countryside magazines that may cover the area. Visit all local booksellers and ask them if they are interested in selling copies at normal trade terms. The usual discount is 33 per cent but W. H. Smith and some other booksellers expect 40 per cent. Most bookshop managers have authority to buy books but not the managers of W. H. Smith's shops, so ask for the name of the Divisional Manager and send him a copy to consider. Send a copy to the County Librarian asking him if he would like to purchase it, mentioning any bookshops which have it for sale. YHA Sales, 29 John Adam Street, London WC1, and the Scout & Guide Shop, Buckingham Palace Road, London SW1, have bookshops and are often interested in selling footpath guides.

If the guide covers a well-known walking area, it is worth trying to get it published by one of the firms specializing in footpath guides. The best known are:

Dalesman Publishing Co. Ltd, Clapham via Lancaster, Lancs. (north of England only)

Footpath Publications, Adstock Cottage, Adstock, Buckingham.

Gerrard Publications, 26 Manor Road, Harrow, Middlesex.

Shire Publications, Cromwell House, Church Street, Princes Risborough, Bucks.

Spurbooks, 6 Parade Court, Bourne End, Bucks.

Bibliography

AUTOMOBILE ASSOCIATION, *No Through Road*, Drive Publications Ltd, 1975.

WAINWRIGHT, ALFRED, *Fellwanderer: The Story behind the Guidebooks*, Westmorland Gazette, 1966.

Appendix 1   ORGANIZATIONS
               OFFERING WALKING
               HOLIDAYS

YHA Adventure Holidays, Department HB, Trevelyan House, St Albans, Herts. Tel. St Albans 55215.

Holiday Fellowship Ltd, Department 342, 142 Great North Way, London NW4. Tel. 01–203–3381.

Ramblers' Holidays Ltd, Wings House, Welwyn Garden City, Herts. Tel. 31133.

The Country-Wide Holidays Association, 24 Birch Heys, Cromwell Range, Manchester M14 6HU. Tel. 061–224–2887. (Provides recreative, educational and health-giving holidays at lowest possible cost. Operates twenty guest houses in Great Britain and overseas.)

Milbanke Travel Ltd, 104 New Bond Street, London W1Y 0AE. Tel. 01-493–8494. (Organizes guided walks along long distance footpaths staying at first-class hotels.)

MAGAZINES AND
PERIODICALS OF
INTEREST TO
WALKERS

Camping Link House Publications Ltd, Dingwell Ave.,
Croydon CR9 2TA. Monthly. Covers all aspects of camping with a regular feature on backpacking. Useful, too,
for news of new equipment.

Climber & Rambler Holmes McDougal Ltd, 36 Tay Street,
Perth. Monthly. Possibly the most civilized of magazines
devoted to walking. Tends to concentrate on climbing
and fell-walking and often adopts a mandarin approach
to the subject. Tests new equipment and has excellent
book reviews and articles. Incorporates *Mountain Life* and
is now the official journal of the British Mountaineering
Council.

Footpath Worker The Rambler's Association, 1/4 Crawford
Mews, York Street, London W1. Published occasionally.
A duplicated news-sheet of great interest to all those concerned in preserving rights of way. Gives detailed information about court cases involving paths.

Practical Camper Haymarket Publishing Ltd, Gillow House,
5 Winsley Street, London W1A 2HG. Monthly. Comprehensive coverage of news of interest to campers together with articles on the subject. Has a regular feature
on backpacking and tests the latest equipment.

The Rucksack The Ramblers' Association, 1/4 Crawford
Mews, York Street, London W1. Three issues per year,
free to members.

The official journal of the Ramblers' Association and
easily the best magazine for walkers. It contains an extremely comprehensive news section covering all matters

relating to paths and the countryside together with well-informed comments on the Ordnance Survey and the amenity and conservation scene in general. Good book reviews and short notices of footpath guides.

Association for the Preservation of Rural Scotland

1 Thistle Court, Edinburgh EH2 1DE. Tel. 031–225–6744.

AIMS: The protection of rural scenery and amenities of country towns and villages of Scotland from unnecessary disfigurement.

Backpackers' Club

Honorary National Organizing Secretary: Eric R. Gurney, 20 St Michael's Road, Tilehurst, Reading RG3 4RP.

AIMS: To ensure continual rights of access to meadow, mountain, woodland, moor and shore. To campaign for, and aid provision of, sections of public footpath and rights of access to these. To encourage, by example and instructions, the full use of the established long-distance footpaths, national parks and open areas.

To campaign and aid the establishment of further similar areas in this country and in the European continent.

To encourage and aid the development of lightweight camping, walking and camping equipment.

British Mountaineering Council

Crawford House, Precinct Centre, Manchester University, Booth Street East, Manchester. Tel. 061–273–5835.

The British Mountaineering Council, founded in 1944, is constituted to foster and promote the interests of British mountaineers and mountaineering in the United Kingdom and overseas. Jointly with the Mountaineering Council of Scotland it is the representative body of British mountaineers. Full membership is open to mountaineering clubs and organizations whose principal objects are mountaineering, who have headquarters in the United Kingdom and who are owned and controlled by their members. Associate membership is open to bodies which do not qualify for full membership, and to individuals.

The work of the BMC includes assisting member clubs and, with their co-operation, improving facilities such as guide books, huts, reciprocal rights in club-huts, ensuring adequate training for novice mountaineers and medium performers wishing to improve their skills, resisting encroachments on the mountain environment, negotiating access rights for mountain areas, outcrops and sea cliffs and helping expeditions overseas in co-operation with the Mount Everest Foundation and the Alpine Club. The testing of a wide range of equipment is organized. Advice on mountaineering matters is given to a wide variety of organizations. In cooperation with the Mountaineering Council of Scotland, the BMC provides a British Mountain Guide qualification for experienced mountaineers who wish to perform as mountain guides in Britain.

BMC publications cover many aspects of mountaineering. They include guide books, safety handbooks, pamphlets and posters, equipment, information and advice. Sets of safety filmstrips or slides covering summer and winter mountaineering are available.

Camping Club of Great Britain and Ireland Ltd

11 Lower Grosvenor Place, London SW1W 0EY. Tel. 01–828–9232.

Looks after camping interests. It has forty-five camping

sites of its own and publishes a directory of 2,500 British and Irish sites.

AIMS: Promotion of knowledge, love and care of the countryside through camping and kindred activities.

JOURNAL: *Camping and Caravanning*.

Has groups devoted to lightweight camping and mountaineering.

The Commons, Open Spaces and Footpath Preservation Society

166 Shaftesbury Avenue, London WC2H 8JH. Tel. 01–836–7220.

The society, founded in 1865, aims to promote knowledge of the law so that paths and commons may be preserved for the public benefit. All walkers have benefited from the excellent work done to preserve rights of way.

Publishes a quarterly journal containing articles and a summary of important legal cases.

Council for the Protection of Rural England

4 Hobart Place, London SWIW OHY. Tel. 01–235–5959

Founded in 1926 the Society exists to protect all that is worthwhile in the English countryside. It recognizes that changes must take place but where they do they should be for the better. The CPRE concerns itself with new housing and industrial development, power stations, overhead transmission lines, new reservoirs and the extraction of water from rivers and lakes, sand and gravel workings, limestone quarrying and opencast coalmining, the felling and planting of trees, the siting of new roads, especially motorways, and the use of land by government departments.

Whenever necessary, the CPRE co-operates with other amenity bodies and lobbies MPs, briefs counsel for public inquiries, and offers advice to government departments and planning authorities.

There are branches in most counties.

Council for the Protection of Rural Wales (Cymdeithas Diogelu Harddwch Cymru)

14 Broad Street, Welshpool, Powys. Tel. Welshpool 2525

AIMS: The protection and improvement of rural scenery and of amenities of the countryside and towns and villages of Wales and Monmouthshire.

Publishes a newsletter.

Countryside Commission

John Dower House, Crescent Place, Cheltenham, Glos. Tel. 21381.

The Countryside Commission is a statutory body set up under the Countryside Act, 1968. It took over the work of the National Parks Commission in running the National Parks and is also responsible for providing grants for public access to open country, wardens, clearing eyesores, making footpaths and nature trails, car parks, lavatories and camping and caravan sites. The Commission also negotiates routes for long-distance footpaths, designates areas of outstanding beauty, provides information centres, helps create country parks and generally provides recreational facilities in the countryside.

Members of the Countryside Commission are appointed by the Secretary of State for the Environment and the Secretary of State for Wales acting jointly.

Countryside Commission for Scotland

Battleby, Redgorton, Perth PHI 3EW. Tel. (0738) 27921.

AIMS: (1) To keep under review all matters relating to the provision, development and improvement of facilities for the

enjoyment of the countryside, the conservation and enhance-
ment of its natural beauty and amenity, and the need to
secure public access to the countryside for the purposes of
open-air recreation; and to consult with such local planning
authorities and other bodies as appear to the Commission
to have an interest in those matters;

(2) to encourage, assist, concert or promote the implementation of any proposals with respect to those matters made
by any other person or body, being proposals which the
Commission considers to be suitable;

(3) to exercise certain functions relating to development
projects or schemes designed to facilitate enjoyment of the
countryside or to conserve or enhance its natural beauty or
amenity;

(4) to consult with local planning authorities regarding
the exercise of their powers under Section 48 of the Act relating to the creation of country parks, and to advise such
authorities thereanent;

(5) to advise the Secretary of State for Scotland or any
other Minister or any public body on such matters relating
to the countryside as he or they may refer to the Commission, or as the Commission may think fit.

English Tourist Board

4 Grosvenor Gardens, London SWIW ODU. Tel. 01–730–3400

AIMS: To encourage the provision and improvement of
tourist amenities and facilities in England, and to organize
publicity within the UK for tourist attractions in England;
to administer schemes of financial assistance to the hotel
industry under Part II of the Act, and to individual tourist
projects.

Regional Tourist Boards

Northumbria Tourist Board, Prudential Building, 140–150
   Pilgrim Street, Newcastle upon Tyne NEI 6TQ. Tel.
   28795

East Midlands Tourist Board, Bailgate, Lincoln LNI 3AR. Tel. 31521

Cumbria Tourist Board, PO Box 2, Windermere, Cumbria.

Heart of England Tourist Board, PO Box 15, Worcester WRI 3QQ.

Yorkshire, Cleveland and Humberside Tourist Board, 312 Tadcaster Road, York YO2 2HF. Tel. 97961

East Anglia Tourist Board, 14 Museum Street, Ipswich IPI IHU.

Thames and Chilterns Tourist Board, PO Box 10, Abingdon, Berkshire OX14 3HG. Tel. 4344

North West Tourist Board, 119 The Piazza, Piccadilly Plaza, Manchester MI 4AN. Tel. 061-236-0393

South East English Tourist Board, Cheviot House, 4-6 Monson Road, Tunbridge Wells TNI INH. Tel. 33066.

West Country Tourist Board, Trinity Court, Southernhay East, Exeter EXI IQS. Tel. 76351

Isle of Wight Tourist Board, 21 High Street, Newport, Isle of Wight PO30 IJS. Tel. 4343

Forestry Commission

25 Savile Row, London WI. Tel. 01-734-4251

The Forestry Commission was established by Act of Parliament in 1924 and has the general duty of promoting the interests of forestry, the development of afforestation, the production and supply of timber and the maintenance of reserves of growing trees in Great Britain. It is responsible for nearly 2 million acres of woodland. The Forestry Commission has some camp sites and operates paths and nature trails.

Long-Distance Walkers Association

Membership Secretary: John Feist, 1 Lowry Drive, Marple Bridge, Stockport, Cheshire SK 6 5BR.

AIMS: To further the interests of those who enjoy long-distance walking by organizing or supporting events and by providing its members with information on organized events and long-distance paths. The LDWA caters for the following kinds of long-distance walking:

(a) organized marathons and events (such as the Fellsman Hike, Tanner's Marathon or Berkshire Ridgeway Marathon);

(b) walks along long-distance footpaths (e.g. the Pennine Way or Cleveland Way) and other open challenges which may be attempted at any time by any individuals or groups – such as the Lyke Wake Walk, the Six Shropshire Summits, or the Three Peaks Walk.

While any of these walks may be regarded as competitive, in the sense that they offer a challenge which others may also be taking up, no emphasis is placed on any form of racing or road walking. Members receive an informative newsletter several times a year giving details of forthcoming events.

Mountain Bothies Association

Hon. Secretary: B. J. Heath, 7 Jim Lane, Marsh, Huddersfield, Yorkshire.

AIMS: The MBA is a voluntary body formed to maintain simple unlocked shelters in remote country for the use of walkers, climbers and other outdoor enthusiasts who love the wild and lonely places.

Mountain Leadership Training Board

Crawford House, Precinct Centre, Manchester University, Booth Street East, Manchester. Tel. 061–273–5839.

The Mountain Leadership Training Board (transferred to and administered by the British Mountaineering Council as from 1 January 1973) was set up in 1964 to provide a scheme of training for the increasing number of leaders who take groups of young people into the mountains. The Board consists of representatives of the Sports Council, the British Mountaineering Council, the British Association of Organizers and Lecturers in Physical Education, the Association of Wardens of Mountain Centres, the Combined Services, the Scottish Mountain Leadership Training Board and the Northern Ireland Mountain Leadership Training Board with observers from the Department of Education and Science and the Mountain Rescue Committee.

Mountain Leadership Certificate

This is the basic award which aims at raising the standard of knowledge and competence of leaders in mountainous country. Minimum age: (a) for registration and on introductory courses, 18 years; (b) for the award of a certificate, 20 years.

To obtain the award a candidate must:

(1) complete an introductory course of at least one week's duration at a training centre approved by the Board; this course is not a beginners' course but an introduction to the MLC. All candidates should be committed hill-walkers or climbers with a substantial recent history of mountainous country activities. *It is not suitable for novices.*

(2) Following this, have at least one year's practical experience as an assistant leader or group member of expeditions during weekends and holidays, details of which must be recorded in a personal log book. This period is designed to allow candidates to prepare for assessment by putting into practice the techniques and theories acquired on the introductory courses; and to provide the assessor with the evidence he needs to carry out a fair assessment;

(3) attend a final week's residential course at an approved centre for assessment;

(4) Be conversant with the following books:
  Safety on Mountains
  The Mountain Code
  Mountain Rescue and Cave Rescue
  Mountain Leadership Handbook

(5) produce a current certificate in First Aid of the St
John Ambulance Brigade or the British Red Cross Society
(Adult Basic 'C').

All candidates for MLC Assessment must be registered
with the MLTB and possess a log book.

Orienteering, mountain rescue, survival and search,
mountain environment, winter mountain courses and rock-
climbing courses provide suitable training for those taking
Leadership and Mountaineering Instructor certificates.

Exemption: Exemption should be applied for when the
candidate, after studying the syllabus and the publications
(paragraph 4), feels confident he is fully conversant with the
requirements. Unjustified exemptions can result in failure at
assessment. A person already experienced in the leadership
of groups of young people in mountainous country may
apply to the Training Board for exemption from the introductory course and also from the period of log-book experience.

Mountainous Country: For the purpose of the certificate,
mountainous country is defined as wild country where the
candidates will be dependent on themselves and remote
from any immediate help. This can be found in the United
Kingdom only in Dartmoor, Exmoor, Brecon Beacons,
Black Mountains, Mid and North Wales, Peak District, Isle
of Man, Pennines, Cheviots, Lake District, North York
Moors, Sperrin Mountains, North Antrim Hills, Mourne
Mountains, Galloway Hills, the Central and Western Highlands, Isles of Skye, Arran, Harris and Lewis.

All registered candidates are eligible for Associate Membership of the British Mountaineering Council. Details available from the address above.

Mountaineering Instructor Certificates

These certificates are a progression from the Mountain
Leadership Certificates. There are two grades:

(1) The Mountaineering Instructor Certificate
(2) The Mountaineering Instructor Advanced Certificate

Training and certification are designed to meet the needs both of permanent instructors employed at mountain centres and of part time or temporary instructors whether employed at mountain centres or on the staffs of schools or youth centres.

Instructor Certificate (Minimum age 18 years): Candidates can be accepted for registration if possessing the MLC summer and winter certificates, or evidence of proficiency supplied by the Warden/Director/Principal of a recognized mountain centre. In exceptional circumstances a candidate may proceed to MIC Assessment without possessing the MLC winter certificate but the MI certificate will not be awarded until the MLC winter certificate is obtained. Orienteering, mountain rescue training, survival and search, mountain environment, winter mountain courses and rock-climbing courses provide suitable training for those taking the Mountaineering Instructor Certificate.

Advanced Certificate: Candidates for the Advanced Certificate must have held the Instructor Certificate for at least one year. Apply to the Mountain Leadership Training Board (or the Scottish or Northern Ireland Boards) for registration and further information.

Mountain Rescue Committee

9 Milldale Avenue, Temple Meads, Buxton, Derbyshire SKI7 9BE.

AIMS: (1) To provide or assist in the provision of mountain rescue equipment with medical and surgical supplies and also rescue posts in the mountains and moorlands of Great Britain.

(2) To see to the proper maintenance and replacement of equipment.

(3) To encourage and assist in the formation of mountain rescue teams where need for them can be shown.

(4) To encourage investigation and experiment in rescue and first-aid methods and to make them known.

(5) To further the cause and to improve the efficiency of mountain rescue in any way.

(6) To represent Mountain Rescue interests to other national bodies.

(7) To raise funds and administer them for these purposes.

Mountaineering Council for Scotland

11 Kirklee Quadrant, Glasgow G12 0TS. Tel. 041–339–7713

AIMS: To promote mountaineering in Scotland.
Publishes a newsletter.

National Trust

42 Queen Anne's Gate, London SW1. Tel. 01–930–0211

The National Trust for Places of Historic Interest or National Beauty was founded in 1895 by Miss Octavia Hill, Sir Robert Hunter and Canon H. D. Rawnsley to halt the destruction of the countryside by the uncontrollable growth of industry. The aim of the National Trust is to educate public opinion and to give people access to the countryside by acting as trustees to the nation by acquiring land and buildings worthy of permanent preservation. The National Trust now owns some 400,000 acres in England, Wales and Northern Ireland and some 200 houses of outstanding architectural or historic importance. It has also accepted covenants which protect against development a further 61,000 acres and many more buildings. Property of the National Trust can never be sold or mortgaged nor compulsorily purchased without consent of Parliament.

National Trust for Scotland

5 Charlotte Square, Edinburgh EH2 4DU. Tel. 031–225–2184

AIMS: To promote the preservation, for the benefit of the nation, of places of natural beauty or historic or architectural interest in Scotland.

Publishes a yearbook giving a directory of all properties.

Ramblers' Association

1/4 Crawford Mews, York Street, London WIH IPT. Tel. 01–262–1477/8

AIMS: To protect the interests of ramblers, and to maintain and extend their rights and privileges; to foster a greater love, use and knowledge of the countryside; to assist in the preservation of countryside amenities, and to maintain friendly relations with landowners and with the rural community generally.

By representations at public inquiries concerning threats to the landscape; by deputations to Government Departments and local authorities; by giving evidence to special committees; by memoranda to Ministers, Members of Parliament and others; by meetings and demonstrations and in many other ways the Association is constantly serving the interests of walkers, mountaineers and all who believe that the beauty of our land should not be heedlessly impaired.

All members receive the Annual Report, *Rucksack* (3 issues yearly), and *Bed, Breakfast and Bus Guide*. They are also free to join in the Area activities of the Association, including lectures, rambles, socials etc. On the other hand, there is no attempt to 'organize' or direct the rambler who likes to walk alone.

Scottish Mountain Leadership Training Board

4 Queensferry Street, Edinburgh. Tel. 031–225–5544

Responsible for administering the Winter Certificate Scheme. The Mountain Leadership Certificate (Winter) is concerned with the very exacting technical skills required for taking parties on to the Scottish mountains under winter conditions. It is equally appropriate elsewhere in the UK whenever similar conditions exist or may be expected. It is an obligatory qualification for candidates for the Instructors' Certificates, for whom it forms an essential part of the training requirements, but it is also open to those who, having gained the Mountain Leadership Certificate (Summer), seek this particular qualification only.

Scottish Rights of Way Society Ltd

32 Rutland Square, Edinburgh EH1 2BZ.

AIMS: (1) The preservation, defence and acquisition of public rights of way in Scotland; and the doing of such acts as may be necessary to preserve or restore such rights of way as may be in danger of being lost.

(2) The erection, restoration and repair of bridges, guideposts, notice or direction boards and plates, fences, stiles, gates and resting places in connection with such public rights of way; and also the repairing of the roads or pathways themselves.

(3) The defence and prosecution, directly or indirectly, of suits or actions for the preservation or recovery of such rights of way.

(4) The doing of all such other lawful things as are incident or conducive to the above objects.

Scottish Tourist Board

23 Ravelston Place, Edinburgh EH4 3EU. Tel. 031–332–2433

Information Office: 2 Rutland Place, Edinburgh EHI 2YU.
Tel. 031–229–1561

Established under the Development of Tourism Act, 1969,
and is responsible for promoting Scotland within Britain and
administering the hotel development incentives scheme. It
gives fundamental assistance to other tourist information
services, carries out research and assists the British Tourist
Authority in publicizing Scotland overseas.

PUBLICATIONS: *Where to Stay in Scotland, Scotland for Hill
Walking*, and various other maps, guides and lists of accommodation.

Scottish Youth Hostels Association

7 Glebe Crescent, Stirling FK8 2JA. Tel. 0786–2821

AIMS: 'To help all, but especially young, people of limited
means living and working in industrial and other areas to
know, use and appreciate the Scottish countryside and
places of historic and cultural interest in Scotland, and to
promote their health, recreation and education, particularly
by providing simple hostel accommodation for them on their
travels.'

The Scottish Youth Hostels Association has a network of
eighty hostels located throughout the country.

Members of other national Youth Hostels Associations
may use Scottish hostels on production of their current
membership card.

Wales Tourist Board

Welcome House, Llandaff, Cardiff CF5 2YZ. Tel. 567701

AIMS: The Wales Tourist Board gives assistance to tourist
projects in Wales, provides tourist information services and
generally promotes tourism in Wales.

PUBLICATIONS: *Where to Stay in Wales, Wales Walking*, and
other tourist publications.

Youth Hostels Association

Trevelyan House, 8 St Stephen's Hill, St Albans, Herts. Tel. 55215

AIMS: 'To help all, especially young people, of limited means to a greater knowledge, love and care of the country-side particularly by providing hostels or other simple ac-commodation for them in their travels, and thus to promote their health, rest and education.'

To achieve these objects more than 250 hostels have been established throughout the country where members can stay. Inexpensive meals are available at most hostels and there are usually facilities for members to cook their own meals. Prices are kept low because members have to do a few household chores before leaving in the morning. The YHA also offers tours and travel services to its members.

JOURNAL: *Hostelling News.*

GLOSSARY

Anorak   A thigh-length garment with a hood which is pulled over the head. It has a short zip and drawstrings and often a kangaroo pocket across the chest. Usually made of polyurethane-coated nylon or, less commonly, closely woven cotton.

AONB   *See* Area of Outstanding Natural Beauty.

Area of Outstanding Natural Beauty (AONB)   Regions of special landscape beauty which have been designated by the Country-side Commission in consultation with the local authority. AONBs have no special administrative arrangements but the local planning authority will usually pay particular attention to controlling development.

Balaclava   A woollen hat which can be fitted round the ears and chin. In good weather usually worn on the top of the head.

Beck   A mountain stream.

Bench mark   A mark usually made by surveyors on a permanent object such as a wall to indicate a known height above sea level.

Benighted   Being stranded on a mountain after dark.

Bivouac hut   A simple structure provided for emergency shelter on mountains.

Bivouac sack (Bivvy sack)   A simple plastic or nylon bag large enough to serve as a tent. It is carried for emergency use in bad weather in the mountains.

Box quilting   A method of sewing duvet clothing and sleeping bags so that there is always a layer of insulating material between two pieces of material holding the insulation in place. This eliminates the cold spots inevitable with simple quilting.

Bridleway   A highway over which the public have a right of way on foot, on horseback and on a pedal bicycle. In Scotland there is no statutory right to use a pedal cycle on a bridleway.

Brocken spectre   A combination of atmospheric conditions which results in the mountaineer seeing his own shadow cast on a wall of cloud or mist.

Burn A mountain stream.

Byway A byway is defined in the Countryside Act, 1968 as meaning 'a byway open to all traffic'.

Cagoule (*Cag*) A knee-length anorak.

Cairn A pile of rocks or stones to mark the summit of a mountain or the route of a path. Invaluable for route-finding in mist.

Chaps The American term for leggings.

Clough A ravine or valley with steep sides especially in the Peak District.

Col *See* Pass.

Combe A narrow valley with grass covered slopes running into the side of a hill. Also used to describe a steep valley running in from the sea, especially in the west country. 'Coomb' and 'coombe' are variant spellings.

Common Land over which some members of the public (but not necessarily the public at large) have certain rights, e.g. the right to graze cattle or gather fuel. Common land always has an owner.

Contour Lines drawn on maps to indicate height and shape of land. See p. 61.

Cornice An overhanging lip of snow on a mountain ridge. Very dangerous to walkers on the ridge, as it can break and plunge down the ridge, carrying the walkers with it.

Corrie A Scottish name for a cwm (q.v.).

Crag A steep and rugged rock.

Crag-fast The condition of being unable to move on a crag or cliff. Walkers should never attempt to climb crags. No attempt should be made to rescue animals or climbers who are crag-fast but help should be summoned from the nearest point.

Crampons Claw-like metal objects strapped on the soles of boots to give better grip on ice and hard snow. Used only by the hardiest of walkers in mountainous country.

Cwm A rounded hollow in a mountain side forming a wall or cliff at one end and with a valley dropping away at the other end. Often there is a tarn or lake in the cwm which feeds a stream.

Definitive Map In England and Wales highway authorities have a legal obligation to publish maps showing rights of way. The inclusion on the Definitive Map of a right of way is conclusive evidence in law of the existence of a right of way unless a diversion or extinguishment has been granted. This applies even if the right of way has been included on the map in error.

Down clothing Jackets, trousers, waistcoats etc. filled with down. Such clothing is exceptionally warm and comfortable but not really necessary in Great Britain except, perhaps, for winter mountaineering in Scotland.

Drove road A route used in times past for driving animals especially cattle and sheep to market.

Dubbin A leather preservative used on boots to keep them supple and water-resistant.

Duvet A down jacket.

Edge A term used particularly in the Peak District and Pennines to describe an outcrop of rock on a ridge forming a vertical face.

Elmslie and English 2,000-footers 348 English summits which exceed 2,000 ft in height. The list was compiled by W. T. Elmslie.

Enclosure A field.

Escarpment A steep slope or inland cliff particularly in chalk country. The steepest part is the scarp and the more gradual slope is the dip.

Exposure The cooling of the body temperature caused by climatic conditions. See pp. 221-4.

Fell Often used in the Lake District and Pennines to describe a mountain. Also used to describe a moor or mountainside.

Fell-walking A term used to describe serious walking in upland areas of the north of England.

Footpath A highway over which the public have a right of way on foot only.

Frostbite Frozen body tissue, especially of the extremities such as fingers, toes, ears and nose. A very serious condition.

Gaiters *See* Stoptout.

Ghyll A mountain stream or ravine, particularly in the Lake District and Pennines.

Gill *See* Ghyll.

Glacier cream A cream used by walkers in snowy conditions to protect the exposed parts of the body from the harmful effects of ultra-violet radiation.

Glen A narrow valley, especially in Scotland.

Glissading A method of descending a snow slope by sliding. Not recommended unless properly taught.

Gorge A very steep-sided narrow valley.

Greasy rock Stones and boulders covered with lichen, moss and grass which is very slippery when wet.

Green roads   Green roads have no statutory definition but they are usually unsurfaced public highways and are often classed as 'Roads Used as Public Paths' or 'byways'.

Grough   A peat bog, especially in the Peak District.

Gully   A ravine made by the action of water.

Hachures   A form of shading on maps to represent the shape of the land.

Hag   A peat bog.

Hanging valley   A valley in a mountainside above the main valley. The stream from the hanging valley usually enters the main valley by a waterfall.

Headland path   A path that follows a field boundary.

Helm wind   The name of the strong north-easterly wind which blows over Cross Fell (2,930 ft), the highest point in the Pennines.

Hill   A summit not exceeding 2,000 ft in height.

Hill-walking   Another name for fell-walking.

Hob nails   Round nails with flat heads in the centre of the soles and heels of boots. Walking boots are rarely nailed nowadays as nails have been largely superseded by hard moulded-rubber soles.

Hoosier   A crude gate made of barbed wire. One end is fixed to a post in the ground. The post at the free end has a loop of wire which can be attached to the fixed post thus allowing the wire to be opened and closed.

Ice axe   Carried by experienced walkers in mountainous country in snowy conditions. It is used for cutting steps in hard snow and ice and as a walking stick for steadying the walker when crossing steep slopes.

Kissing gate   A small gate hung in a U- or V-shaped enclosure.

Knott   An outcrop of rock frequently found in the Lake District.

Ladder stile   A stile over a wall or fence giving access by means of several steps.

LDP   *See* Long-Distance Path.

Long-Distance Path (LDP)   A path for long-distance walkers created and approved by the Countryside Commission.

Moor   High ground usually covered in heather.

Mountain   A summit over 2,000 ft.

Mountain rescue posts   These are located in suitable places such as huts, hotels, police stations and farms. They are usually, but not always, on the telephone and contain first-aid equipment and a stretcher. Often marked on Ordnance Survey maps.

Mountain rescue teams   Volunteers who undertake rescue work.

They are usually members of the walking and climbing fraternity living locally who give their services free.

Muggers A generic name for clinker and hob nails. Rarely used nowadays by walkers, as nails have been superseded by moulded-rubber soles.

Munro tables A list of Scottish mountains over 3,000 ft compiled by Sir Hugh Munro.

Nails Once fitted to walking boots but now almost completely superseded by moulded-rubber soles.

Naismith's formula A method of calculating the time necessary to walk a certain distance in mountainous country. Allow one hour for every three miles covered, plus half an hour for every thousand feet climbed.

National Park Areas of mountain, moor, heath, down, cliff or foreshore containing a high proportion of open country which have been designated as National Parks by the Secretary of State for the Environment.

Needle A tall sharp rock or crag found particularly in the Lake District.

Outcrop A small cliff on a mountain.

Pack-frame A light-alloy frame carried on the shoulders and secured at the hips to which may be attached a sac for carrying kit and equipment.

Parka A fur-lined anorak.

Pass Low ground between two mountains which provides easy access to the next valley. Sometimes called a col.

Peak The summit of a mountain.

Peat Vegetable matter especially heather and bracken decomposed by water and often forming bogs and marshes.

Pike The name given to pointed mountains in the Lake District.

Ravine A pronounced cleft in a mountainside.

Ridge A narrow line with the mountainside falling steeply away on either side.

Road Used as Public Path (RUPP) 'A highway, other than a public path, used by the public mainly for the purpose for which footpaths or bridleways are so used' (National Parks and Access to the Countryside Act, 1949). Under the Countryside Act, 1968 RUPPs are to be reclassified as byways open to all traffic, bridleways or footpaths.

Rucksack A bag used for carrying kit and equipment. It is supported on the back by straps that pass over the shoulders. It may or may not be used with a pack-frame (q.v.).

RUPP   *See* Road Used as Public Path.

Saddle   A broad dip between two areas of higher ground in mountainous country.

Scar   A cliff or rock face on a mountainside usually formed by a geological fault.

Scarp   *See* Escarpment.

Scramble   Very easy climbing, without rope, on broken rocks.

Scree   Areas of small stones on steep mountain sides found particularly in the Lake District.

Scree-running   The art of running down a scree by digging the heels into the loose stone rather similar to running down shingle on a beach. Most screes in the Lake District are now badly worn by constant use.

Sleeping bag   An insulated bag used by campers instead of blankets.

Snow-blindness   Temporary blindness caused by ultra-violet rays in mountainous country.

Snow goggles   Special goggles worn in the mountains to protect the eyes from snow glare and ultra-violet rays.

Spot height   Heights shown on Ordnance Survey maps.

Spur   A projection from a mountain.

Stile   A structure usually consisting of one or two steps giving access through a fence or hedge.

Stoptout   Gaiters that fit over the boots and up the calf. They are useful in keeping the legs dry in wet weather and snow. They will also keep small stones from lodging inside the boots.

Tarn   A mountain lake.

Tor   A hill or rocky peak. Used particularly on Dartmoor and in Cornwall.

Triangulation pillar (*Trig point*)   A stone or concrete pillar erected by the Ordnance Survey to mark an exact height established by surveying instruments.

Tricouni nails   Nails with sharp edges useful for obtaining grip on rough rock. Now almost completely superseded by moulded-rubber soles.

Trig point   *See* Triangulation pillar.

Verglas   A thin coating of ice on rocks which makes walking very dangerous.

Waymark   A symbol indicating a path. Some waymarks indicate direction of path.

White-out   Mist on a snow covered mountain which makes it difficult to distinguish features on the ground.

INDEX

(Place names given passing mention have not been indexed)